Organizations Express

John Middleton

T0313455

- ■ Fast track route to understanding what makes organizations tick

- ■ Covers the key areas of achieving organisational effectiveness, from building core skill sets and mastering the impact of technology and globalization, to aligning culture with direction and developing new organizational models and structures

- ■ Examples and lessons from some of the world's most successful businesses, including Dell, Nissan, Semco and St Luke's, and ideas from the smartest thinkers, including Charles Handy, Elliott Jaques, Arie de Geus and Ricardo Semler.

- ■ Includes a glossary of key concepts and a comprehensive resources guide.

essential management thinking at your fingertips

The right of John Middleton to be identified as the author of this work has been asserted in accordance with the Copyright, Designs and Patents Act 1988

First published 2002 by
Capstone Publishing (a Wiley company)
8 Newtec Place
Magdalen Road
Oxford OX4 1RE
United Kingdom
http://www.capstoneideas.com

CIP catalogue records for this book are available from the British Library and the US Library of Congress

ISBN 1-84112-230-0

FSC
Mixed Sources
Product group from well-managed
forests and other controlled sources

Cert no. SGS-COC-2953
www.fsc.org
© 1996 Forest Stewardship Council

Contents

Introduction to ExpressExec

ExpressExec is 3 million words of the latest management thinking compiled into 10 modules. Each module contains 10 individual titles forming a comprehensive resource of current business practice written by leading practitioners in their field. From brand management to balanced scorecard, ExpressExec enables you to grasp the key concepts behind each subject and implement the theory immediately. Each of the 100 titles is available in print and electronic formats.

Through the ExpressExec.com Website you will discover that you can access the complete resource in a number of ways:

» printed books or e-books;
» e-content – PDF or XML (for licensed syndication) adding value to an intranet or Internet site;
» a corporate e-learning/knowledge management solution providing a cost-effective platform for developing skills and sharing knowledge within an organization;
» bespoke delivery – tailored solutions to solve your need.

Why not visit www.expressexec.com and register for free key management briefings, a monthly newsletter and interactive skills checklists. Share your ideas about ExpressExec and your thoughts about business today.

Please contact elound@wiley-capstone.co.uk for more information.

Introduction to Organizations Express

» Uncertain times for organizations.
» Sources of guidance.
» "Nothing fails like success."

"Thirty years ago I started work in a world-famous multinational company. By way of encouragement they produced an outline of my future career. 'This will be your life,' they said, 'with titles of likely jobs.' The line ended, I remember, with myself as chief executive of a particular company in a particular far-off country. I was, at the time, suitably flattered. I left them long before I reached the heights they planned for me, but I already knew that not only did the job they had picked out no longer exist, neither did the company I would have directed, nor even the country in which I was to have operated."

Charles Handy, The Age of Unreason (Hutchinson, 1989)

For organizations there are no certainties any more. Size is no guarantee of business success – ask Marconi, the electronics company whose value plummeted by 97% in a few weeks in 2001 on the back of difficult markets and poor management. Longevity and reputation guarantee nothing – just ask Marks & Spencer what has happened to their customer base over the past five years. Innovation and enthusiasm can count for little – observe the burnt out shells of the hundreds of dotcoms that have gone out of business.

And these are not just isolated examples. Life is getting more challenging for every organization. The impact in recent times of new technology and globalization is that your company's biggest competitor and potential nemesis could be huge or tiny, and could be based around the corner or on the other side of the world.

These then are dangerous times and, as a consequence, organizations have never seemed so fragile or ephemeral. On average, they are around for less than the equivalent of one human generation. So where can we turn if we want to give our own organizations the best possible chance of success?

To other companies? Certainly, we can learn from the success of other organizations but how and what we learn is another matter. It isn't enough to simply replicate the good practice of others and expect the formula to work perfectly in our own organizations. Imitation may be the sincerest form of flattery, but simple mimicry is a mindless strategy.

To academics, consultants and other so-called "experts?" By all means, take regular soundings of other people's views about where the business world is heading but be sure to make up your own mind. A McKinsey study of AT&T in the early 1980s predicted that "the total market for mobile cellular phones will be 900,000 subscribers by the year 2000." Based on that original McKinsey assessment, AT&T decided to pull out of the market, only to re-enter it at great expense through the purchase of McGaw in the 1990s. In these volatile times, don't rely on anybody else's view of the future.

One thing is for sure. Even if we manage to locate the formula for organizational success, it will be a formula with a sell-by date. As Richard Pascale once put it so memorably: "Nothing fails like success."

And so there is nothing in *Organizations Express* that will guarantee the long-term survival of any organization. Our goal, and this is as good as it gets, is to give you the chance to get momentarily ahead of the game.

Good luck!

What is an Organization?

We all have an instinctive sense of what organizations are because most of us either work in one of them or provide services or products to them. There are any number of definitions of an organization. This section takes our understanding of organizations to a deeper level by looking at fundamental questions.

» What is an organization?
» What is organization development?
» What is organizational behavior?

"The power business has over our lives is awesome. It can promote us or dump us. It can offer self-esteem or lack of dignity. It can frighten and coerce us. It can stretch our imaginations. It can destroy families and it can sponsor and build marriages."

Andy Law, chairman of St Luke's advertising agency, London

We all have an instinctive sense of what organizations are because most of us either work in one of them or provide services or products to them. And yet, depending on where you look and whom you ask, there are any number of definitions of an "organization," some of which follow.

» Organizations are social arrangements for achieving controlled performance in the pursuit of collective goals.
» Organization coordinates many parts into a whole, which helps people to do things more efficiently and harmoniously.
» Organizations are merely conceptual embodiments of a very old, very basic idea – the idea of community.
» They can be no more or less than the sum of the beliefs of the people drawn to them: of their character, judgments, acts, and efforts.
» Organizations are interesting places but – given the choice – you wouldn't want to work in one.

Of these, the first definition is perhaps the most illuminating. It was coined by David Buchanan and Andrzej Huczynski in their book *Organizational Behavior*[1]. The key phrase is "controlled performance", which the authors define as "setting performance standards, measuring actual performance, comparing actual with standard, and taking corrective action if necessary."

Organizations are set up to achieve something. The "something" may change over time and will vary significantly from organization to organization, but there is a sense of underlying purpose as an organization tries to adapt to changes in its external environment.

To take our understanding of organizations and organizational phenomena to a deeper level, we need to start drawing on some of the many conceptual frameworks that have evolved over the last century or so. Broadly speaking, the study of organizations has broken down into two key fields: organization development and organizational behavior.

ORGANIZATION DEVELOPMENT

The term "organization development" (or OD, the label most commonly used in the field) has been in use since at least 1960. There are many individual definitions of the term. An all-encompassing definition of OD is as follows.

OD is an effort that is:

1 planned;
2 organization-wide; and
3 managed from the top; to increase
4 organizational effectiveness and health; through
5 planned interventions in the organization's "processes," using behavioral-science knowledge.

To break the definition down to those five elements:

1 *Planned:* an OD intervention requires the systematic diagnosis of the organization, the development of a strategic plan for improvement and the mobilization of resources to carry out the effort.
2 *Organization-wide:* an OD effort is related to total organization change (change the culture, reward systems or strategy) rather than tactical efforts. A system need not be a total corporation but must be free to determine its own plans and future within general environmental constraints.
3 *Managed from the top:* an OD effort requires active participation by top management who must have knowledge and commitment to the goals of the program.
4 *Designed to increase organizational effectiveness and health:* there are numerous measures of organizational effectiveness and health. Some are: how work is managed against goals and plans; whether form follows function (the problem, task or project determines how resources are organized); whether decisions are made by or near the sources of information (regardless of the organization chart); does the reward system ensure that managers (and supervisors) are rewarded for appropriate achievements.
5 *Planned interventions:* OD is not about haphazard, off-the-cuff actions – it is about taking measured action.

ORGANIZATIONAL BEHAVIOR

Organizational behavior (OB) is generally defined as the study of human behavior, attitudes and performance *within* an organizational setting. OB draws on theory, methods and principles from such disciplines as psychology, sociology, and cultural anthropology to learn about individual perception, values, learning capabilities, and actions while working with groups and within the total organization.

WHERE TO BEGIN?

The management bookshelves are weighed down by literally thousands of books and journals, which are designed to help people understand the workings of organizations a little better. Faced with this overwhelming choice, most consultants and internal change agents tend to compile their own anthology of preferred gurus, models, and frameworks.

The reader will need to find their own sources of illumination but here are two people who are particularly worth exploring.

Elliott Jaques

A key figure in illuminating our understanding of what organizations are about is Elliott Jaques, visiting research professor in management science at George Washington University.

For over 50 years, Jaques has consistently advocated the need for a scientific approach to understanding work systems. He argues that there is a "widespread, almost universal, under-estimation of the impact of organization on how we go about our business." He believes, for example, that rapid change in people's behavior is achieved less through altering their psychological make-up and more by revising organizational structures and managerial leading practices.

His book *Requisite Organization*[2] challenges many current assumptions about effective organizations, particularly in the field of hierarchy, of which Jaques is a fan. Some may find his theories indigestible, but for those who persist with studying the theories below there is a wealth of challenging material that undermines much conventional organizational wisdom.

» *Assumed organization:* the pattern of connections between roles as it is assumed to be by the different individuals who occupy positions in the organization.

» *Extant organization:* the pattern of connections between roles as shown by systematic research to be actually operating.

» *Manifest organization:* the structure of an organization as it appears on the organization chart.

» *Requisite organization:* the pattern of connections which ought to exist between roles if the system is both to work efficiently and to operate as required by the nature of human nature and the enhancement of mutual trust.

Gareth Morgan

Gareth Morgan, distinguished research professor at York University in Toronto, where he teaches at the Schulich School of Business, offers another framework in his fascinating book *Images of Organization*[3]. Morgan suggests that it is metaphor and analogy that can provide a set of lenses for understanding organizations. In the book, he explores a range of metaphors, looking at:

» organizations as machines;
» organizations as organisms;
» organizations as brains;
» organizations as cultures;
» organizations as political systems;
» organizations as psychic prisons;
» organizations as flux and transformation; and
» organizations as instruments of domination.

Metaphors offer a distinctive means of filtering information about organizations. While there is no one right answer, viewing organizations as machines, or as biological systems, can provide some new insight about the nature of those organizations.

However, there is a danger. Although a new metaphor – organizations as chaotic systems for instance – may initially present a new and fresh view, the nature of the insight is inevitably partial and incomplete. A new metaphor rapidly becomes as limiting a mindset as the more established, traditional metaphors.

NOTES

1. Buchanan, D. & Huczynski, A. (1997) *Organizational Behavior*, Prentice Hall, Hemel Hempstead, UK.
2. Jaques, E. (1997) *Requisite Organization* (revised), Cason Hall & Co., Gloucester, MA.
3. Morgan, G. (1997) *Images of Organization* (2nd ed), Sage Publications, Newbury Park, CA.

The Evolution of Organizations

To understand how organizations have evolved this section looks at the following.

» The early history of organizations.
» Organizations over the last century.
» Key figures: Henri Fayol, Frederick Taylor.
» Key influences: the impact of technology and globalization.

The year is 1901. We're in London. In your hands, you're holding a copy of the newly published London Post Office Directory (the Yellow Pages of its day). As you flick through its pages, you see many of the trades of the day listed. Prominent among them are ash collectors, blood dryers, ice merchants, lamplighters, livery stable keepers, mourning hatband makers, saddlers, soap makers, soot merchants, spermaceti (whale oil) refiners, and starchers.

Fast forward. The year is now 2001. We're in Bristol, England. Not that it matters – we're surfing the net so we might as well be anywhere in the world. We go to the Website for Electronic Yellow Pages. We use the site's search facility to enter all those trades we noted above from the London Post Office directory. Not one has survived intact.

Just look at what's happened to the world of work over the past one hundred years or so: mass production; the rise of "organization man;" the technological explosion of the sixties; mainframes; personal computers; the decline of manufacturing; business re-engineering; outsourcing; downshifting; portfolio workers; globalization; the fall of "organization man" amid a dramatic fall in job tenure; the shortage of knowledge workers; the ascent and descent of the dotcoms; and that's not to mention 101 other phenomena that have shaped organizational thinking and behavior over the years. To paraphrase Fatboy Slim, "We've come a long way, baby."

The roots of twentieth century organizations can be traced back to models of Chinese military hierarchy of a good 2000 years' vintage, and quite probably beyond that too, especially if you extend your search parameters into the natural world. Our concept of "paid work," however, dates back only three hundred years or so to England's Industrial Revolution. Up until that point the world was overwhelmingly rural, and the distinction between work and home largely meaningless.

Increasing numbers of organizations arose in the mid-nineteenth century following the emergence of the concept of limited liability. Specialist merchants and traders developed vertically integrated firms to co-ordinate the increasingly multifunctional operations required to harness the technology and communications advances spurred by the Industrial Revolution.

What industrialization was to the eighteenth and nineteenth centuries, management was to the twentieth. Perhaps more than anybody, Henri Fayol (1841-1925), a mining engineer and manager by profession, defined the nature and working patterns of the twentieth century organization. In his book, *General and Industrial Management*, published in 1916, Fayol laid down what he called 14 principles of management.

Fayol also defined the core principles governing how organizations worked and the contribution of management to that process. He was the first to suggest that management was a discipline in its own right and the first to recognize that the core activities of management were universal, replicating themselves across organizations large and small, across industries, and across national boundaries. He characterized the activities of a commercial organization into six basic elements: technical; commercial; financial; security; accounting; and management.

HENRY FAYOL'S 14 PRINCIPLES OF MANAGEMENT

1 Division of work: tasks should be divided up with employees specializing in a limited set of tasks so that expertise is developed and productivity increased.

2 Authority and responsibility: authority is the right to give orders and entails enforcing them with rewards and penalties; authority should be matched with corresponding responsibility.

3 Discipline: is essential for the smooth running of business and is dependent on good leadership, clear and fair arguments, and the judicious application of penalties.

4 Unity of command: for any action whatsoever, an employee should receive orders from one superior only; otherwise authority, discipline, order and stability are threatened.

5 Unity of direction: a group of activities concerned with a single objective should be co-ordinated by a single plan under one head.

6 Subordination of individual interest to general interest: individual or group goals must not be allowed to override those of the business.

7 Remuneration of personnel: may be achieved by various methods but it should be fair, encourage effort, and not lead to overpayment.

8 Centralization: the extent to which orders should be issued only from the top of the organization is a problem which should take into account its characteristics, such as size and the capabilities of the personnel.

9 Scalar chain (line of authority): communications should normally flow up and down the line of authority running from the top to the bottom of the organization, but sideways communication between those of equivalent rank in different departments can be desirable so long as superiors are kept informed.

10 Order: both materials and personnel must always be in their proper place; people must be suited to their posts so there must be careful organization of work and selection of personnel.

11 Equity: personnel must be treated with kindness and justice.

12 Stability of tenure of personnel: rapid turnover of personnel should be avoided because of the time required for the development of expertise.

13 Initiative: all employees should be encouraged to exercise initiative within limits imposed by the requirements of authority and discipline.

14 *Esprit de corps*: efforts must he made to promote harmony within the organization and prevent dissension and divisiveness.

At the same time as Fayol was bringing clarity of definition to the concept of management, Frederick W. Taylor, "the father of scientific management" and arguably the world's first management consultant, was actively taking ideas about how organizations could be most efficiently managed into the workplace.

His work with car-making legend Henry Ford led directly to the mass production techniques that created 15 million Model Ts between 1910 and 1927, and that set the pattern for industrial working practice world-wide. Taylor advocated the use of time-and-motion study as a means of analyzing and standardizing work activities. His scientific approach called for detailed observation and measurement of even the most routine work, to find the optimum mode of performance.

Although he lived through little of it – he died in 1915 – Taylor's influence on the twentieth century is unquestionable. Peter Drucker, for example, rates him alongside Freud and Darwin as a maker of the modern world. And despite its critics, Taylorism and the production methods that it spawned in the early part of the twentieth century, lives on, whether in the form of re-engineering (a direct descendant of scientific management), the continuing debate about the de-skilling of many jobs, or the standardized global practices of companies like McDonald's.

SCIENTIFIC MANAGEMENT: TAYLOR'S FIVE SIMPLE PRINCIPLES

1 Shift all responsibility for the organization of work from the worker to the manager; managers should do all the thinking relating to the planning and design of work, leaving the workers with the task of implementation.
2 Use scientific methods to determine the most efficient way of doing work; assign the worker's task accordingly, specifying the precise way in which the work is to be done.
3 Select the best person to perform the job thus designed.
4 Train the worker to do the work efficiently.
5 Monitor worker performance to ensure that appropriate work procedures are followed and that appropriate results are achieved.

In his biography of Taylor, *The One Best Way* (Little Brown, 1997), Robert Kanigel neatly sums up Taylor's impact on the world of work.

"The coming of Taylorism made our age what it was going to become anyway – only more so, more quickly, more irrevocably. Taylor died relatively young. But he lived long enough to take currents of thought drifting through his own time – standards, order, production, regularity, efficiency – and codify them into a system that defines our age. In its thrall, and under its blessing, we live today."

Because the industrialists of the early decades of the twentieth century followed Henry Ford's lead and put the emphasis on efficiency, it was some years before any significant attention was paid to the needs and motivations of that other major factor involved in the work process – the workers. One of the early pioneers of a view that actually people were central to the world of business was Mary Parker Follett (1868–1933). Although she has achieved an almost legendary status since her death, her views were largely ignored at the time by the business world.

However, the seeds were sown, and a number of people setting up businesses in the 1930s – people like Bill Hewlett and Dave Packard, for instance – began to realize that the nature of the relationship between a company and its workforce impacted explicitly on the quality of contribution that individuals made. Treat people with respect and bear their needs and interests in mind, and they typically make a better contribution. Treat them as production fodder, and they park their brains outside before walking through the gates of the company and into work.

The workplace of the first half of the twentieth century, then, was dominated by efficiency-obsessed Taylorism, accompanied by a slowly growing realization on the part of some organizations that extracting the optimal performance out of people required a more subtle understanding of the human heart and mind.

During the second half of the last century, organizations had to cope with two additional influences, namely the impact of new technology, and the globalization of the economy.

THE IMPACT OF NEW TECHNOLOGY

If you're a fan of horror movies, you'll know one particular device used by directors to trick audiences: lead them into expecting a gruesome shock; build up the tension as the music swells; the door creaks open slowly to reveal . . . nothing. And then, wham, out jumps the bogeyman.

When computers were brought into companies for the first time, predominantly in the 1960s, it was a bit like that. A lot of money was invested over a long period but, fundamentally, nothing changed.

There was no significant increase in productivity, and neither were there significant job losses. And then, wham!

Particularly during the 1980s, it became more and more apparent that the real bottom line of technology was that it made jobs go away. It didn't happen all at once. But, starting in the manufacturing industries and then moving into white-collar work, every day more work was being automated. And both the white-collar workplace and the factory floor were transformed.

As companies gained more technological savvy, they became less tied to time or place, and less reliant on a large, permanent workforce. Against this backdrop, the notion of lifetime employment in one company all but disappeared.

THE GLOBALIZATION OF THE ECONOMY

One of the UK's pre-eminent historians, Eric Hobsbawm, has written extensively about life since the Industrial Revolution. Although the scope of his books goes well beyond organizations, work and careers, he provides some brilliant insights into how these elements fit into the broader economic and social picture. So here's Hobsbawm writing in his book *The New Century* (Little Brown, 2000) on the topic of globalization.

"We are certainly a single global economy compared with thirty years ago, but we can say with equal certainty that we'll be even more globalized in 2050, and very much more in 2100. Globalization is not the product of a single action, like switching on a light or starting a car engine. It is a historical process that has undoubtedly speeded up enormously in the last ten years, but it is a permanent, constant transformation. It is not at all clear, therefore, at what stage we can say it has reached its final destination and can be considered complete. This is principally because it essentially involves expanding across a globe that is by its very nature varied geographically, climatically, and historically. This reality imposes certain limitations on the unification of the entire planet. However, we are all agreed that globalization, and especially the globalized economy, has made such spectacular progress that today you couldn't talk of an international division of labor as we did before the seventies.''

Of course, globalization and technology are inter-connected phenomena. Technology is the prime enabler of a globalized economy. In her book *The Death of Distance* (Orion, 1997), Frances Cairncross gives some examples of how this interplay manifests itself:

» *The death of distance:* distance no longer determines the cost of communicating electronically. Companies are increasingly able to organize certain types of work in three shifts according to the world's three main time zones: the Americas, East Asia/Australia, and Europe.

» *The fate of location:* no longer is location key to most business decisions. Companies can locate any screen-based activity anywhere on earth, wherever they can find the best bargain of skills and productivity. Many developing countries now offer on-line services – monitoring security screens, running help-lines and call centers, writing software, and so forth.

» *More minnows, more giants:* on one hand, the cost of starting new businesses is declining, and so more small companies are springing up to provide services that, in the past, only giants had the scale and scope to provide. Individuals with valuable ideas, initiative, and strong business plans can attract global venture capital and convert their ideas into viable businesses. On the other hand, a seemingly relentless wave of mergers and takeovers are reducing many industry sectors to a handful of huge, global players. Charles Handy sums up these twin phenomena thus: ''It's obviously going to be a different kind of world ... It will be a world of fleas and elephants, of large conglomerates and small individual entities, of large political and economic blocs and small countries.''

SO WHERE ARE WE NOW?

Life, as we know, is rarely neat. If the impact of technology and the globalization of the economy were the two key themes of the latter part of the twentieth century, it's clear that these themes are far from being fully played out. They will continue to be the dominant shapers of who does what type of work where.

We can, however, draw some broad conclusions about the state of organizations and the working world.

Traditional jobs still exist – but not here

As Kevin Kelly has put it, "The old economies will continue to operate profitably within the deep cortex of the new economy." The fact is that around the world there are just as many cars and ships being constructed as ever, just as many roads being built, just as much coal being produced, as much steel being made. Eric Hobsbawm writes that it is a mistake to talk of a post-industrial era, because in reality those goods and services that were produced in the industrial era are still being produced today. The difference is where they are now being produced. "Traditional" industries are all thriving "somewhere else" in the world.

The local labor exchange has become a global job market

Manufacturing capacity will continue to shift from Western economies to those countries with access to cheaper labor. Equally, technology is allowing more and more knowledge-based work to be shipped to the cheapest environment. This may bring jobs to emerging economies but can create severe pressures for unskilled workers in more advanced economies.

White collars will continue to feel the pinch

Tom Peters has predicted that 90% of white-collar jobs in the US will either be destroyed or altered beyond recognition in the next 10 to 15 years. As he puts it, "That's a catastrophic prediction, given that 90% of us are engaged in white-collar work of one sort or another."

The home as office

As more of us work from home, the line between work and home life will blur. Home design will also change, and the domestic office will become a regular part of the house.

The bottom line is that the world of work has changed irrevocably

The collective impact of globalization and technology is that no organizations can claim protected species status. If there is a cheaper or better quality alternative to a company's products and services anywhere in the world, that company is at risk. Darwin was right: if you can't outpace your environment, you're doomed.

The E-Dimension

We have never seen anything like the Internet; it is having enormous impact on organizations. This section explores the key issues and questions.

- » The Internet's high-speed impact on business.
- » How technology has changed the way that organizations and their people work.
- » Ten Internet business principles.

"We thought the creation and operation of Websites was mysterious Nobel Prize stuff, the province of the wild-eyed and purple-haired. Any company, old or new, that does not see this technology as important as breathing could be on its last breath."
Jack Welch, former chairman of General Electric, quoted in The
Observer, May 14, 2000.

"Technology, globalization, the shift toward services – are breaking down the old social contract, leaving workers at the mercy of a new and ruthless variety of capitalism."
Stan Davis, Future Perfect (1987).

"Politicians still pretend they can conjure up new jobs for the huge number of soon-to-be-employed. When will they ever learn that technology is the problem not the solution? Today, productivity is delivered by a technology needing only a few machine minders. Growth is created from the intellect of knowledge workers not from the labor of low-grade service and production workers. Growth has been de-coupled from employment."
Professor Ian Angell of the London School of Economics writing
in Time Manager International's house magazine, Tempus,
Issue 15, 1998.

In terms of speed and depth of impact, our planet has never experienced anything quite like the Internet. Other great transformative technologies – railways, electricity, the telephone, the automobile, and so on – took decades to achieve the kind of critical mass that the Internet has attained in a handful of years.

The new information technologies that have brought dotcom businesses into being are simultaneously restructuring global markets and whole industry sectors, challenging conventional economic thinking, redefining how business is done, and impacting to varying degrees on every worker in the global marketplace.

Sometimes the present is best understood when viewed from the past. The last big social change in work – the Industrial Revolution – destroyed some ways of life but also made it possible for many people to live far better than ever before. So while agricultural laborers found their jobs disappearing, new and differently skilled jobs sprang up in factories. This phenomenon had a resonance in the late twentieth century as people in manufacturing industry found their skills were becoming redundant, displaced by the rise of the service industry sector with its knowledge workers, whose primary talent lies in their ability to develop and manipulate ideas.

Peter Drucker, as ever, has captured this phenomenon in a few choice words: "The traditional factors of production – land, labor and capital – are becoming restraints rather than driving forces ... Knowledge has become the central, key resource that knows no geography. It underlies the most significant and unprecedented social phenomenon of this century. No class in history has ever risen as fast as the blue-collar worker and no class has ever fallen as fast. All within less than a century."[1]

This unprecedented speed of change has inevitably led to organizations having to "learn as they go," with little time possible for considered reflection. The result has been organizational carnage, with a huge increase in the number of job losses and business failures over the past few years. For many organizations, the Internet has proved to be more of a graveyard than a gravy train.

There will be a benefit down the line as the lessons behind those failures are absorbed. And perhaps we should be grateful for those early e-business pioneers. As Michael Mark, president and creative director of Matthews/Mark has put it: "Let's stop kicking the carcasses of the fallen dotcoms. They're the heroes of the front lines, on whose boldness and *naïveté* we will one day feed our children."[2]

To date, most attention has been focused on the snazzy business models underpinning e-businesses. Less has been said about how the Internet impacts on organizations and – lest we forget – the people who work in them. So what has been the explicit impact? How is organizational life now different to say, 20 years ago?

This is easier to ask than answer. All too often, we absorb the impact of technology without really noticing the difference. Mobile phones are now taken for granted – ten years ago they were nowhere to be seen. Before the invention of the electric light by Thomas Edison, people slept an average of 10 hours a night. Today, we sleep on average for 7.1 hours, with a third of people getting by on less than six hours.

WHAT DOES IT ALL MEAN?

One thing is clear. The impact of information technology on organizations has already been significant and can only increase over the coming years. Directly or indirectly, technology is redefining the nature of organizations and work. New computer-based systems dissolve all organizational conventions of ownership, design, manufacturing, executive style, and national identity.

Here are just a few of the ways in which technology has changed the way that organizations and their people work.

Instant global news, instant global impact

News, ideas and information travel faster. Profits at investment banks, airlines, and the wider tourist industry collapsed in the immediate aftermath of America's terrorist attacks. Lay-offs and job cuts followed rapidly.

The paradox of location

Location is becoming a less important factor in business decision-making. Geography matters less . . . and more. Less because:

» location is becoming a less important factor in business decision-making;
» companies are locating screen-based activity wherever they find the best deal in terms of skills and productivity; and
» developing countries increasingly perform on-line services – running telephone help-lines and call centers, writing software, and so on.

But location also matters more because we are seeing a growing phenomenon in places like Silicon Valley, where businesses are, to use a term coined by Michael Porter, "clustering" because the benefits of proximity to competitors outweigh the costs. These perceived benefits include:

» new technology that improves the productivity of the industry as a whole gets diffused more easily;
» it can be easier to pick up on new trends in what buyers want; and
» the effects of competing for employees are balanced by the fact that qualified people from all over the world gravitate to your cluster.

Nine to five becomes 24/7

Companies now organize certain types of work in three shifts according to the world's three main time zones: the Americas, East Asia/Australia, and Europe. The "working day" has no meaning in a global village where electronic communication can happen at any time of day or night.

Size matters less

Small companies can now offer services that, in the past, only giants could provide. What's more, the cost of starting new businesses is declining, and so more small companies will spring up. Many companies will become networks of independent specialists; more employees will therefore work in smaller units or alone. Individuals with valuable ideas can attract global venture capital. Perhaps one of the most telling features of the new economy is that increasing numbers of people can describe themselves without irony as one-person global businesses.

Winners and losers

Driven by the impact of technology and the increased levels of global competition it has enabled, the notion of lifetime employment in one company has all but disappeared. For every empowered, de-layered, nano-technology worker doing valuable work, there is another who has lost their job, and yet another tucked away in their technologically Neanderthal office putting in longer and longer hours, adding less and less value and looking increasingly doomed.

There are bound to be winners and losers in this process but where will it all end? Are we destined to live in a world where some people are permanently overworked while others are permanently underworked?

Customer service is changing

Enquiries and orders handled over the telephone today can be managed over the Internet as a matter of course, at a considerably lower cost. In the US, it costs $1 to process a typical bank transaction in the conventional way; on the Internet, the cost is just one cent.

Short-term focus becomes even shorter

Institutional investors and brokers' analysts have become very demanding of public companies. In the United States in particular, they relentlessly demand an improvement in results every quarter. Fail to deliver against this expectation and top managers are out, regardless of their past track record. Against this backdrop, companies have become reluctant to make long-term investments for fear of damaging their short-term results.

The Internet levels the playing field

Companies that believe that flashy Internet start-ups cannot threaten their core activities built up over years of careful planning, research, branding and marketing are wrong. The Internet is helping to put small agile newcomers on a par with large corporations and able to compete head on with them for new business.

People as the ultimate scarce resource

The key challenge for companies will be to hire and retain good people, extracting value from them, rather than allowing them to keep all the value they create for themselves. A company will constantly need to convince its best employees that working for it enhances each individual's value.

Organizational structures are shifting

As Shoshana Zuboff has written, "Unlocking the promise of an information economy now depends on dismantling the very same managerial hierarchy that once brought greatness."[3]

Give yourself a job

As people in white-collar industries are displaced by automation, they will increasingly work for themselves. Companies will simultaneously outsource more and more and hire people like sub-contractors. Both trends are pointing in the same direction. Nicholas Negroponte has predicted that by the year 2020, the largest employer in the developed world will be "self."[4]

GERRY MCGOVERN'S TEN INTERNET BUSINESS PRINCIPLES

Gerry McGovern has spoken, written and consulted extensively on Web-related issues over the last eight years. In October 2000, he received the Web Ireland Internet Industry Person of the Year award. The following set of principles is derived from his 1999 book *The Caring Economy*.

1 Care. Care about your customers. Care about your staff. Care about all those connected with you. Put people first because people are where you will find your unique competitive advantage.

2 Empower all those connected with you and where appropriate create communities that allow you to organize around the consumer, rather than around a product or service offering.

3 Champion and focus on old people, women and children who are three key engines in The Caring Economy. Also, focus on niches and communities of interest, delivering unique products and services. In the digital age, it will pay to specialize.

4 Focus on the value you deliver, not just the costs you save. Remember, the Internet is not cheap to develop for, requiring quality brands, quality people and substantial ongoing investment.

5 Let your information flow by focusing on the three properties of information: content, structure and publication. Use information quickly and gain value from the momentum it creates.

6 Keep the communication of your information as simple as possible. Cut through the hype and don't fall into the trap of being complicated in a complex age.

7 Think digital and study the lessons that are being learnt in software development. Learn from the Internet too. Remember, the best way to succeed on the Internet is to imitate how the Internet itself became a success and this means thinking network.

8 Learn to play, challenge the unchallengeable, think the unthinkable and encourage the heretic. Evangelize and bring other people with you. Embrace change and flow with the age.

9 Protect and build your brand and good name. Trust is not easy to establish on the Internet and those who gain the consumer's trust will reap the long-term rewards.

10 Have a long-term vision of where you want to go. Don't forget the information-poor consumer. Remember that we are citizens of an increasingly connected world. For the long-term stability and prosperity of our world, we cannot continue to ignore the injustice, poverty and famine that so many of our fellow citizens must daily endure.

LET'S KEEP THINGS IN PERSPECTIVE

The new economy supplements the traditional economy; it does not supplant it. As Kevin Kelly has put it, "The old economies will continue to operate profitably within the deep cortex of the new economy."[5] The fact is that around the world there are just as many cars and ships being constructed as ever, just as many roads being built, just as much coal being produced, as much steel being made. It is a mistake to talk of a post-industrial era, because in reality those goods and services that were produced in the industrial era are still being produced today. The difference is where they are now being produced. Although in the UK Indian restaurants may employ more people than the steel, coal mining and ship building industries combined,[6] "traditional" industries are all thriving elsewhere in the world.

And to finish on a note of reason, here's historian Eric Hobsbawm on the impact of new technology:

"Information technology is certainly producing considerable changes in work. I am skeptical about the possibility of radical change, just as I am skeptical about the ability of the modern economy to operate without any kind of reference to social traditions. Obviously, it is technically possible to work from home and communicate with the world solely by e-mail. The reality is that this is not the way people want to work. Even the high-tech pioneers do not live scattered across the United States and Great Britain, but are concentrated in certain areas where they can meet and communicate. It is not very comforting for human beings not to have someone to speak to, and to renounce personal contacts. This is an absolutely essential element for productivity and efficiency at work. All this talk about decentralized domestic work is partly a good bit of propaganda to justify redundancies. British Telecom is preparing to free itself of 10% of its workforce on the assumption that they will be able to work from home. Besides, it is a case of technological utopianism that ignores the fact that human beings don't want to be on their own, but prefer to work with others."[7]

NOTES

1 Peter Drucker interviewed in *Wired* magazine in July 1993.
2 From an interview in *Fast Company*, May 2001.
3 Shoshana Zuboff writing in *Scientific American*, September 1995.
4 Negroponte, N. (1995) *Being Digital*, Alfred A. Knopf, New York.
5 Kelly, K. (1998) *New Rules for the New Economy*, Fourth Estate, London.
6 As reported in *The Times*, May 18, 2000.
7 Hobsbawm, E., (2000) *The New Century*, Little Brown, London.

The Global Dimension

As a term "globalization" was first coined in the 1980s and this chapter discusses the issues for organizations. It covers:

- » a brief history of globalization;
- » a definition of globalization;
- » five myths;
- » globalization and organizations;
- » globalization and employment; and
- » globalization and the issues for organizations.

"The power of globalization is not about leveraging economies of scale. It's about leveraging economies of knowledge and coordination – figuring out how not to reinvent the wheel everywhere you do business, how to benefit from knowledge created and knowledge shared."

Martin Sorrell, advertising executive, chairman and CEO of WPP Group plc.

"Of all the factors of production, the need for human beings is constantly diminishing. This is because, relatively speaking, they don't produce as much as they cost. Human beings were not created for capitalism. This does not produce negative effects on production, but only on human beings."

Eric Hobsbawm, historian and writer.

Globalization has had a mixed press in recent times: on the one hand resented and denounced, most forcibly at the demonstrations during the World Trade Organization meeting in Seattle in November 1999; on the other hand seen as desirable and, in any case, inevitable.

However, globalization is not just a recent phenomenon. The term was first coined in the 1980s, but the concept stretches back decades, arguably centuries, if you count the trading empires built by Spain, Portugal, Britain, and Holland.

Some people have argued that the world was just as globalized 100 years ago as it is today, with international trade and migration. But the worldwide depression of the 1930s put a temporary end to that, as nation states came to realize that international markets could sometimes engender poverty and unemployment.

WHAT IS GLOBALIZATION?

Globalization is an economic process, the result of human innovation and technological progress. It refers to the increasing integration of economies around the world, particularly through trade and financial flows. The term sometimes also refers to the movement of people (labor) and knowledge (technology) across international borders.

The aftermath of World War II laid the groundwork for today's globalization as the Western states sought once again to build and strengthen international ties in the hope of securing a long-term peace. In more recent times, the Internet's coming of age coupled with advances in telecommunications technology have resulted in a much higher level of cross-border business activity.

Critics say that the industrialized West's gain has been at the expense of developing countries. The already meager share of the global income of the poorest people in the world has dropped from 2.3% to 1.4% in the last decade.

There are also those who argue that what we're experiencing is not just the globalization, but rather the Americanization, of the world economy, with a global consumer culture being spread by companies like McDonald's and Coca-Cola. Less visibly, the global market for all of the main professional services – auditing, accounting, consulting, investment banking – are dominated by American companies.

FIVE MYTHS ABOUT GLOBALIZATION

In their book *A Future Perfect: The Challenge and Hidden Promise of Globalization*[1], John Micklethwait and Adrian Wooldridge outline five myths associated with globalization. This collective "globaloney," as they term it, is dangerous because it can lead to actions that inject misery into the lives of millions:

Myth #1: size trumps all

It doesn't. National champions find it easier to spread globally, but they often encounter other giants when they do. In addition, technology and deregulation of capital markets have made it easier for small companies to upset bigger rivals.

Myth #2: universal products triumph

"Most people have begun to realize that in marketing, just as in navigation, treating the world as if it is flat can have draw-backs." In fact, only a handful of global brands sell everywhere to everyone – and even those brands are sold in different ways in different places.

Myth #3: economics need to be rewritten

Yes, computers and globalization are having an impact on productivity – allowing for fast growth with low inflation. But ultimately, cheap commodities, a strong dollar, and weak labor have more likely caused the long boom of the 1990s.

Myth #4: globalization is a zero-sum game

Yes, there are losers. But overall, globalization creates jobs because it's more efficient. Adam Smith's division of labor still applies: productivity improves when people specialize in what they do best.

Myth #5: geography is disappearing

Geography still matters, because in a global economy, business clusters are important. Relationships also matter, as do shipping times.

GLOBALIZATION AND ORGANIZATIONS

Transnational corporations are companies that operate in more than one country at a time. They have become some of the most powerful economic and political entities in the world today. Many of these corporations have more power than the nation-states across whose borders they operate. For example, the combined revenues of just General Motors and Ford – the two largest automobile corporations in the world at the time of writing – exceed the combined gross domestic product (GDP) for all of sub-Saharan Africa. The revenues of the top 500 corporations in the United States equal about 60% of the country's GDP. Overall, fifty-one of the largest 100 economies in the world are corporations.

Partly as a result of their size, transnational corporations tend to dominate in industries where output and markets are concentrated in the hands of a relatively small number of companies. For example, the top five car and truck manufacturers are responsible for nearly 60% of worldwide sales of motor vehicles. The five leading oil majors account for over 40% of that industry's global market share. For the chemicals sector, the comparable percentage is 35%, and for both electronics and steel it is over 50%.

Over the past quarter century, there has been a virtual proliferation of transnationals. In 1970, there were some 7000 parent transnationals, while today that number has jumped to 38,000. Some 90% of them are based in the industrialized world, and control over 200,000 subsidiaries.

Whatever anybody thinks of globalization, one thing is for sure: it's here. Globalization has become ingrained in our assumptions and in our behavior. Unless we make an effort to find out, we don't really know where our car, computer, Gap sweater or latest CD was made. And by and large, we don't really seem to care. Until, that is, the company we work for decides to shift its production lines overseas to one of the low-wage economies and suddenly it's our job that's at risk.

GLOBALIZATION AND EMPLOYMENT

There is clear evidence that global companies have been eliminating jobs in their home countries and shifting production abroad. Between 1982 and 1993, for example, US transnationals cut over three-quarters of a million jobs at home but added 345,000 jobs outside the United States. Even business folk behind small firms have sympathy for the movement, afraid as they are that global economies of scale will put them out of work.

In those less-industrialized regions, the offer of lower costs and less regulations can all too often come at the cost to local workers of having to forego decent working conditions, sufficient pay, and job security.

GLOBALIZATION: ISSUES FOR ORGANIZATIONS

There are plenty of ways in which globalization can impact on organizations, no matter what their size or industry sector. Which of the following might affect you?

» Sources of competition: your biggest competitor could now be anywhere in the world.

» In a world of instant communication, it's harder to innovate. Product improvements get copied at light speed.

» With the rise of the Web (don't forget that it's the "World Wide" Web), new channels of distribution, and entirely new business models, are being created faster than ever before. Traditional assumptions about strategy, pricing, and selling are under fierce attack. The Web threatens to turn every industry upside down and inside out. We are also seeing the internationalization of business practices, with techniques like business process engineering now being deployed globally. Today Harvard Business School, tomorrow just about anywhere.

» Global management has to be multicultural. The best global companies take the best skills and ideas from wherever they are in the world.

CASE STUDY: HOW ADVERTISING AGENCY WPP FINDS ITS GLOBAL TALENT

Martin Sorrell, 54, chairman and CEO of WPP Group plc, has enjoyed a bird's-eye view of the changing logic of global competition. Here, in an interview[2] published in *Fast Company* magazine, he responds to a question asking him to identify the most serious weakness plaguing big, global companies – American or otherwise.

"The battle for talent. Let's start with our business. As an industry, advertising is simply not getting its fair share of outstanding young people. The really talented people are going into investment banking, into consulting, or into Silicon Valley start-ups. They just don't find the advertising business to be very compelling.

"Why is the ad business losing the battle for talent? Because it doesn't try hard enough. It doesn't commit the resources or the attention that Goldman Sachs, McKinsey, and Andersen Consulting are willing to commit to that battle.

"At WPP, we've been taking steps to compete more effectively. Five years ago, for example, we started the WPP Fellowship Program. We recruit the best of the best for a three-year tour of duty, including one year in each of three different WPP companies. A recruit might spend a year in London with J. Walter Thompson, a year in San Francisco doing market research with Millward Brown, and a year in New York doing PR with Hill & Knowlton. We've received 5000 applications for a program that has just 50 slots per year. But do you know what I find most surprising about this fellowship program? That it's generated so little response from our competitors.

"But don't get the wrong idea: the talent question doesn't just affect our business. There are big, global companies in every industry that seem to operate on an inhuman scale. Young people come into an organization, look up at the heights they have to ascend, and wonder if they'll ever get there. And there continues to be major resistance in big companies to giving young people responsibility early on. I understand that sentiment: if you've just spent 30 years climbing to the top of an organization, your attitude is going to be, 'Other people should serve the same apprenticeship that I did.' You're not going to be very sympathetic to the idea that a 30-year-old can do your job as well as you can.

"If that's how you feel, don't be surprised when talented people from Stanford or Kellogg or Harvard Business School flock to Silicon Valley. Everyone has heard of Moore's Law - the proposition that computer chips will keep getting faster and cheaper over time. There's a Moore's Law of generations too: Younger people are so much more at ease with digital technologies than older people - they relate so much more naturally to the Web - that the difference between someone in his or her fifties and someone in his or her twenties can be absolutely profound.

"Oracle, working with a couple of our companies, recently surveyed senior European executives about their attitudes toward the net and toward digital technology. How big an impact did they expect those things to have on their business? How up to speed did they feel? On the whole, these executives had quite a relaxed attitude. There was no real sense of urgency. I think that the roots of this attitude are generational. Most people who run big European companies are in their 50s or early 60s. They're going to be retiring in five or 10 years. Why would they want to mess with radical change at this stage of their career? Of course, as Nicholas Negroponte of the MIT Media Lab likes to say, the next generation of leaders is just three five-year plans away from taking power.''

NOTES

1 Micklethwait, J & Wooldridge, A, (2000) *A Future Perfect: The Challenge and Hidden Promise of Globalization*, Heinemann, London.

2 Taylor, W. "Whatever happened to globalization?'', *Fast Company*, Issue 27, September (1999).

The State of the Art

To understand the state of organizations today we must give attention to several key elements. This section examines:

- » Turbulent times for organizations.
- » Organizations: big is beautiful?
- » Organizations: small is beautiful?
- » The new pioneers.
- » Organizations: are the best built to last?
- » Organizations: old is beautiful?
- » Organizations in an age of paradox.
- » The impact of demographics.
- » More ideas and concepts in brief.

"The ability to perceive or think differently is more important than the knowledge gained."

The late David Bohm, physicist, quoted in New Scientist,
February 27, 1993

"In the industrial age, information was like gold. In the digital age, it is like milk – use it quickly."

Consultancy NUA's advertising slogan, quoted in Information
Strategy, September 1998

It is a conceit of each passing business generation to imagine that they have to contend with the toughest trading and working conditions ever known. Compared to now, we say, didn't our parents have it easy back in the 60s, the 70s, the 80s . . .

Doubtless, children of the current business generation will have legitimate reasons for feeling they merit the accolade, but even they might concede that, looking back, the first decade of the twenty-first century was a particularly turbulent period.

Turbulent because many of the certainties that used to underpin business life have vanished. Perhaps for any of us of working age, the biggest adjustment we are personally having to make relates to the disappearance of the "job for life." Work hard, keep your job? Don't bank on it.

This turbulence is also apparent in the sheer volume of business ideas and techniques now on offer. The business airwaves are awash in books, articles, conferences, and videos exhorting the modern manager to take on board the latest big ideas: the application of complexity theory to business; lessons behind the rise and fall of the dotcoms; the ripped up psychological contract between organization and individual; the balanced scorecard; managing in a downturn; the end of loyalty; the return of loyalty; emotional intelligence; the narcissistic leader; and so on.

What is clear is that there is no single big theme currently dominating organizational thinking. According to Charles Handy, we are in the age of unreason, a time "when the future, in so many areas, is to be shaped by us and for us; a time when the only prediction that will hold true is that no predictions will hold true."[1]

This section of *Organizations Express* will explore a handful of the emergent ideas and concepts clamoring for managerial attention. Some will certainly prove to be substantive; others may be cul-de-sacs. Some may appear to flatly contradict others – this is, after all, an age of paradox. All will hopefully provoke your thinking. Reflect, discuss, and beyond that, trust your judgment.

ORGANIZATIONS: BIG IS BEAUTIFUL?

"Size matters" proclaimed posters advertising the 1998 movie *Godzilla*. And certainly the latest wave of mergers, acquisitions, and strategic alliances seem to suggest that the future belongs to the corporate giants. On the other hand, the view that big is beautiful has looked less and less convincing in recent times as corporate giants have consistently been upstaged and out-thought by smaller, nimbler rivals.

Robert Baldock, author of *The Last Days of the Giants?*[2], sees major problems ahead for those organizations that have come to believe that their sheer size will protect them from the unpredictability of the next few years. "The environment in which the culture of 'bigness' blossomed is fast disappearing in many industries," he says.

However, the question mark in the title of Baldock's book is significant – the corporate giants of the late twentieth century may be in serious trouble but he believes they can survive in the intensely competitive environment of the twenty-first century if they radically alter the way they do things. He highlights three areas in particular where the giants may need to change their outlook.

1 *The nature of what they offer to their customers:* most companies have traditionally sold products or services to their customers. Increasingly companies will need to think in terms of selling solutions and, beyond that, of satisfying customer intentions. An intention, explains Baldock, is "a desire or goal that may take a person many years to achieve and may involve the integration of products and solutions from multiple firms spanning many industries. For example, 'having an enjoyable retirement' could involve a move to a sunny climate, a new hobby, making financial provisions for your nearest and dearest, and so on." The further a company can move away from simply selling products and services towards providing solutions and

satisfying intentions, the better it will be able to differentiate its offerings from the competition's.

2 *The nature of the relationship they have with their customers:* is the business seller-driven, customer-centric, or buyer-driven? Historically, large organizations have presumed to know what the market might want to buy. More recently, the world has become more customer-centric with sellers trying to tailor their offerings to meet fast-changing consumer needs. Baldock predicts that "we are entering a buyer-driven era, an era in which the customer will not just be a king, but a dictator."

3 *Their level of virtualization:* at the first level, the company tries to do everything in-house. At the second, the company selectively outsources work to third parties. Beyond the outsourcing model lays the virtual enterprise, carrying very few processes itself and concentrating its efforts on organizing the efforts of others. Baldock defines virtualization as "the removal of constraints of form, place and time made possible by the convergence of computing, communications and content."

Combining these three elements, the optimal twenty-first century organization, says Baldock, will be a buyer-driven virtual enterprise that satisfies consumer intentions. His prescription for big business survival involves three stages.

1 Companies should re-assess the economics of sales and delivery channels with a view to dumping excess baggage.

2 They should move to a more customer-centric business model "where their pared-down products and distribution channels are integrated and closely aligned with the key buyer values of their customer segments."

3 They must turn their business model through 180 degrees in order to come up with value-creating packages that satisfy consumer intentions.

Whether Baldock truly has come up with a route map for big business survival is open to question, but *The Last Days of the Giants?* is necessary bed-time reading for any large company CEO whose business is in danger of being taken to the cleaners by upstart dotcom competitors.

ORGANIZATIONS: SMALL IS BEAUTIFUL?

A growing share of some of the fastest growing sectors of the British economy is accounted for by a new and independent breed of cultural entrepreneurs. Across Britain, thousands of young people are working from bedrooms and garages, workshops and run-down offices, hoping that they will come up with the next Hotmail or Netscape, the next Lara Croft, the next Wallace and Gromit or *Notting Hill*.

This group, labeled "the independents" by Charles Leadbeater and Kate Oakley in a pamphlet[3] from independent think tank, Demos, are typically in their twenties and thirties and have emerged from a convergence of three forces.

1 Technology: this is the first generation that grew up with computers and that understand how to reap the benefits of modern computing power and communications. In earlier decades, increased computer power primarily benefited large organizations. The independents feel enabled, not threatened, by new technology.
2 Values: the independents are typically anti-establishment, anti-traditionalist and highly individualistic. Those values pre-dispose them to pursue self-employment and entrepreneurship in a spirit of self-exploration and self-fulfillment.
3 Economics: they have entered the workforce from the late 1980s onwards, during which time self-employment and entrepreneurship have become very attractive alternatives to careers in large, impersonal, frequently downsizing organizations.

Leadbeater and Oakley go on to offer some advice for aspirant independents.

» Be prepared to have several goes: you're unlikely to make it first time around. Learn from failure, don't wallow in it.
» Timing is critical: technology is moving so fast it's easy to be either too early or too late.
» Don't have a plan: it will come unstuck because it's too inflexible.
» Have an intuition and a feel for where the market is headed: adapt and change with the consumers.
» Be brave enough to be distinctive: if you are doing what everyone else is doing, you're in the wrong business.

» Be passionate: if you don't believe in what you are doing, nobody else will. At the outset only passion will persuade other people to back you.

» Make work fun: if it stops being fun, people will not be creative.

» Give your employees a stake in the business: you may not be able to pay them much to start with so give them shares.

» Pick partners who are as committed as you: to start with, a business will only be sustained by a band of believers.

» Don't be sentimental: be ready to split with your partners – often your best friends – when the business faces a crisis or a turning point.

» Create products that can become ubiquitous quickly: for example by being given away in a global market, thereby attracting huge stock market valuations.

» Don't aim to become the next Bill Gates: aim to get bought out by him.

» Take a holiday in Silicon Valley: you will be convinced anyone is capable of anything.

The independents are a growing group of people who value creativity and openness over more traditional career routes. Although they do not aspire to work in big business, the irony is that they represent one of the best potential sources of jobs and growth for others.

THE NEW PIONEERS

In the US, a growing number of small- and medium-size firms are achieving spectacular success. At the heart of these firms' successes, says Tom Petzinger[4], is an entrepreneurial outlook that is team-rather than self-centered. An open, selfless organization is not only good for the business, but also good for of all involved, both inside and outside. Such an organization needs people who are individually passionate about what they do and but who use all of their resources for the good of the team and the wider company.

Petzinger puts forward a compelling case for small and medium sized businesses being the engine room of a new economy more often characterized as being populated by mega-corporations at one end of the scale or tiny start-ups at the other. At a deeper level, he is arguing for a fundamental shift in our collective thinking about the nature of organizations. Few people wake up on a Monday morning positively enthused about the prospect of going into work. And yet Petzinger has uncovered hundreds of small companies where people have a genuine desire to belong and to contribute, where individual capability is harnessed to a collective potential to create astonishing results.

ORGANIZATIONS: ARE THE BEST BUILT TO LAST?

When the best-selling business book *Built to Last*[5] appeared in 1994, it was the product of a six-year investigation by James Collins and Jerry Porras, both Stanford professors at the time, which set out to uncover the underlying principles that could yield enduring, great companies. For the book they examined 18 companies that had significantly outperformed the general stock market over a number of decades. The companies looked at included Disney, General Electric, Hewlett-Packard, IBM, and Wal-Mart.

The key finding to emerge from their research was, in their words: ''The fundamental distinguishing characteristic of the most enduring and successful corporations is that they preserve a cherished core ideology while simultaneously stimulating progress and change in everything that is not part of their core ideology. Put another way, they distinguish their timeless core values and enduring core purpose (which should never change) from their operating practices and business strategies (which should be changing constantly in response to a changing world).''

For Collins and Porras the essence of greatness does not lie in cost cutting, restructuring, or the pure profit motive. It lies in people's dedication to building companies around a sense of purpose and around core values that infuse work with the kind of meaning that goes beyond just making a profit. Truly great companies, they claim, immerse their people in the core ideology. At Disney, for example, where workers are ''cast members'' rather than employees, the language and day to day rituals of the organization act as an ongoing reinforcement of the values of the company.

But the clinching argument for them is in the evidence they found that those companies with a strong core ideology and which opted to make a lasting contribution also make more money than their more pragmatic, short-termist rivals in the end.

Implicit on every page of *Built to Last* is a simple question: why would a company settle for creating something mediocre that does little more than make money, when it could create something outstanding that makes a lasting contribution as well? At a time when it seems the lifespan of some dotcom companies can be measured in weeks or months rather than decades, this question strikes at the heart of business and life in the new economy.

Even as Collins and Porras were preparing their findings in the early 90s, in fact since the 70s, entrepreneurs have followed a Silicon Valley paradigm – a set of assumptions about how to handle a start-up. The model is very simple: come up with a good idea, raise venture capital, grow as quickly as you can, and then go public or sell up. Above all, though, do it at speed. Even 20 years ago, a company that hadn't made it big within 7 to 10 years was deemed a failure. There was also at that time an ethic of impermanence: the Silicon Valley business culture generally had no expectation that a company would be built to last.

By today's standards of short-termism Silicon Valley-style, that time frame seems positively snail-like. By today's standards, entrepreneurs like Bill Hewlett and Dave Packard, co-founders of Hewlett-Packard, or Sam Walton, founder of Wal-Mart, look like relics of a bygone business era.

Aware that much of what is currently going on in the new economy seems to undermine the validity of the findings of *Built to Last*, James Collins faced the criticism head-on in an article he wrote for Fast Company magazine provocatively titled *Built to Flip*[6]. In the article, he tells a story that gives an insight into the twenty-first century entrepreneurial mindset:

> "Not long ago, I gave a seminar to a group of 20 entrepreneurial CEOs who had gathered at my Boulder, Colorado, management lab to learn about my most recent research. I tried to begin with a quick review of Built to Last findings, but almost immediately a chorus of objections rang out from the group: 'What does 'building to last' have to do with what we face today?"

Built to Flip is an intriguing idea. As Collins describes it: "No need to build a company, much less one with enduring value. Today, it's enough to pull together a good story, to implement the rough draft of an idea, and, presto! – instant wealth. In the built-to-flip world, the notion of investing persistent effort in order to build a great company seems, well, quaint, unnecessary – even stupid.''

He goes on:

> "Have we labored to build something better than what members of previous generations built – only to find their faces staring back at us in the mirror? Is the biggest flip of all the flip that transforms the once-promising spirit of the new economy back into the tired skin of the old economy?''

Encouragingly, he concludes that *Built to Flip* is itself not built to last. He puts his faith in a combination of the underlying logic of the marketplace and the nature of the human spirit:

> "Built to Flip can't last. Ultimately, it cannot become the dominant model. Markets are remarkably efficient: in the long run, they reward actual contribution, even though short-run market bubbles can divert excess capital to non-contributors. Over time, the marketplace will crush any model that does not produce real results. Its self-correcting mechanisms will ensure the brutal fairness on which our social stability rests.''

Let's hope that Collins is right. Let's hope that founders of new economy businesses come to realize that it is better to concentrate primarily on building an organization rather than on hitting a market just right with a visionary product idea and riding the growth curve of an attractive product cycle. Let's hope that the primary output of their efforts is the tangible implementation of a great and sustainable idea and that their greatest creation is the company itself and what it stands for.

ORGANIZATIONS: OLD IS BEAUTIFUL

Arie de Geus worked for 38 years at Royal Dutch/Shell where he was heavily involved in scenario planning. In the early 1980s the Shell Group undertook a study into corporate longevity. The study found that long-lived companies have four essential traits in common.

1 Sensitivity to the environment – a company's ability to learn and adapt.
2 Cohesion and identity – a company's innate ability to build a community and persona for itself.
3 Tolerance and decentralization – a company's ability to build constructive relationships with other entities, within and outside itself, and a willingness to experiment.
4 Conservative financing – a company's ability to finance its own growth and evolution effectively by retaining resources that enable flexibility.

In his book *The Living Company*[7], Arie de Geus draws a sharp distinction between "living companies" whose purpose is to fulfill their potential and perpetuate themselves as ongoing communities, and "economic companies," which are in business solely to produce wealth for a small inner group. He likens managers in living companies to stewards who understand that keeping the company alive means handing it over to a successor in at least the same health that it was in when he or she took charge.

Here are some other key points and insights from *The Living Company*.

Value people not assets

This inversion of normal managerial priorities was supported in Shell's study by the fact that each of the 27 long-lived companies selected changed its business portfolio at least once.

Loosen the steering and control

By definition a company that survives for more than a century lives in a world that it cannot hope to control. A policy of tolerance enables a company to diversify without courting disaster, by allowing it to continually engage with its environment without damaging its capacity for growth.

Organize for learning

In order to help us understand how an organization (as opposed to an individual) learns, Arie de Geus quotes the work of Allan Wilson at the

University of California at Berkeley on how species learn. Wilson states that three conditions are necessary to aid species learning.

1 The members of the species must have and use the ability to move around, and they must flock or move in herds rather than sit individually in isolated territories.
2 Some of the individuals must have the ability to invent new behaviors, new skills.
3 The species must have a process for transmitting a skill from the individual to the entire community, not genetically but through direct communication.

The presence of these three conditions serves to accelerate learning in the species as a whole, increasing its ability to adapt quickly to fundamental changes in the environment.

Share the human community

Managers who want to build an organization that can survive many generations pay attention to the development of employees above all other considerations. In organizations in which benefits accrue to only a few people, all others are outsiders not members. According to their underlying contract with the company, those outsiders trade their time and expertise for money – and that type of contract does not inspire loyalty. Recruits understand that they should work with their eventual exit in mind.

ORGANIZATIONS IN AN AGE OF PARADOX

It doesn't seem that far back in the corporate timeline when change used to happen in bursts, if at all. Occasionally, if you remember, a new CEO would have a rush of blood and personally re-design the business on the back of attending an executive seminar, or perhaps bring in some consultants to help. Senior managers would sigh, brace themselves for a few bumpy months, and look forward to a time when life in the company would settle down again. Then, around about the mid- to late 1980s, it dawned on companies that "change was a constant" and that organizational life would never be quite the same again.

And now, with constant change absorbed as an unquestioned given on most corporate agendas, post-millennial business life in the hinterlands of the new economy is due for another shake-up, say Watts Wacker and Jim Taylor in their book *The Visionary's Handbook*[8]. Forget constant change, and embrace what the authors call constant paradox – a continuous collision of opposites that will affect us and the terms of our business and personal lives every moment we are alive.

In fact, Wacker and Taylor set out nine paradoxes in all, covering everything from value and time to competition, action, leadership and leisure.

THE NINE PARADOXES

The paradox of value: intrinsic worth isn't

The value of any product becomes inseparable from a buyer's perception of worth. Instead of intrinsic value, we have relative value only – the products that a business makes bear diminished relations to the physical content of the offering.

The paradox of size: the bigger you are, the smaller you need to be

To operate effectively in a world in which each individual is a micro-culture and to communicate effectively and directly to the interests of those micro-cultures, you have to, in effect, atomize your organization and miniaturize its units.

The paradox of time: at the speed of light, nothing happens

To succeed in the short term, you need to think in the long term. Yet the greater your vision and the longer the time interval over which you predict results, the greater the risk that you will be unable to take the necessary steps in the short term to achieve the long-term goals. The tension between short- and long-term planning has never been more tormented.

The paradox of competition: your biggest competitor is your own view of your future

Competition comes from everywhere and nowhere at the same time. Competition needs to be viewed in both external and internal terms. Competition takes place in all three tenses.

The paradox of action: you've got to go for what you can't expect to get

Nothing will turn out exactly as it's supposed to. You must act intuitively and be equally ready to take resolute counterintuitive action.

The paradox of leadership: to lead from the front, you have to stay inside the story

In an inherently inconsistent world, consistency is not the virtue it once was in our leaders.

The paradox of leisure: relax, dammit; play is hard work

Play and work are blending and becoming indistinguishable.

The paradox of the visionary: our reality is yours alone

The closer your vision gets to a provable truth, the more you are simply describing the present. In the same way, the more certain you are of a future outcome, the more likely you will be wrong

The paradox of reality: your reality is ours alone

Every person on planet earth today has the potential to be connected to every other person, and every single one of us inhabits a world of our own and is a marketing segment of absolutely one. As our links become stronger, our individuation becomes starker.

There are no glib, pre-packaged ways to resolve these paradoxes. And for organizations more used to dealing in simplistic either/ors, this would be a failing. However, as we come to recognize the growing complexity of the working world, we will necessarily need to become attuned to some of the apparent paradoxes that it throws up.

DEMOGRAPHICS AND THE ORGANIZATION

Throughout history, societies have been extraordinarily young, with an average age of around 20. Within our lifetime, we will see that average rise to 50 in the West. Not only will the age balance shift, but populations in many countries are set to decline. In the late 1990s Japan became the first country ever with an average age of 40; in 2007 its population will reach a peak and then start falling. Italy will follow soon after, and by 2025 there will be more Italians aged over 50 than under that age. Populations in Europe are poised to plunge on a scale not seen since the Black Death in 1348.

The demographic changes will have an impact globally. They will also have an impact on some key areas relevant to organizational life, as in the following examples.

» The future *can* be viewed optimistically with the weight of numbers battering down ageism in the workplace and allowing people to work longer and more flexibly. However, if anything, the smaller numbers of young people available for work will start bidding wars for their services – scarcity, not glut, confers power in markets.

» The waves of downsizing and down-layering from the 1990s are likely to continue as companies shake out a perceived excess of middle-aged managers The opportunities for many older workers will lie as subcontractors to large companies, whether as individual freelancers or by setting up their own small businesses.

» State pensions stand in the demographic firing line: in many countries pension promises are unaffordable and will have to be broken. The alternative is a quite unacceptable escalation in contributions, over-burdening the much smaller working population that will have to find the resources to honor these promises.

All countries in the West will find their weight in the world diminishing. Favorable demographics will foster fast progress in developing countries, while many western countries will be hit by declining labor forces.

[This section was derived from ideas set out in *Agequake* by Paul Wallace (Nicholas Brealey Publishing, New York, 1999).]

ORGANIZATIONS: A FEW MORE IDEAS AND CONCEPTS IN BRIEF

A good business model is not enough

The rise and fall of dotcoms left markets reeling and CEOs scratching their heads. The most important lesson from this whole debacle: ignore basic economic principles at your own risk. Technology changes. Economic laws do not.

Working with emotional intelligence

According to Daniel Goleman, the originator of the term, emotional intelligence does not mean merely being nice; rather, it means "managing feelings so that they are expressed appropriately and effectively, enabling people to work together smoothly toward their common goals."[9] Organizations have not been noted for their level of emotional intelligence over the years. Command and control companies doubtless thought it a wishy-washy nicety. However, as organizations adopt more conciliatory management patterns, it's becoming clear that what's important about people is not just their individual skills but also the relationships they form with one another. By investing in this "social capital," companies can often push their performance to a whole new level. There is an old-fashioned word for this growth in emotional intelligence: maturity.

Managing complexity – the appliance of science

Organizations are finding valuable food for thought in the scientific fields of complexity and chaos theory as they come to realize that links between causes and effects are more complex than simple linear systems can capture. This carries some practical implications for orga-nizations. For example, because the long-term future is unknowable, organizations should stress adaptability, creativity and entrepreneur-ship. And complexity theory also casts some doubt over the value of long-term planning processes, suggesting instead that organizations require structures which encourage self-transformation not detailed plans for long-term futures.

Managing know-how

There are many who argue that knowledge management or intellectual capital will be the foundation of corporate success in the new century. If companies are set to stand or fall by their management of their intellectual capital (defined by Thomas Stewart, an early writer on the topic, as "packaged useful knowledge"), then their ability to develop appropriate systems and to provide a setting within which people will be willing to share their knowledge (rather than hoard it in the fear that sharing knowledge makes them more dispensable) becomes a crucial organizational challenge.

NOTES

1 Handy, C. (1989) *The Age of Unreason*, Hutchinson, London.
2 Baldock, R. (2000) *The Last Days of the Giants?* Wiley, New York.
3 Leadbeater C. & Oakley, K. (1999) *The Independents: Britain's New Cultural Entrepreneurs*, Demos, London.
4 Petzinger, T. (1999) *The New Pioneers*, Simon and Schuster, New York.
5 Collins, J. & Porras, J. (1994) *Built to Last*, HarperCollinsBusiness, New York.
6 Collins, J. (March 2000) "Built to flip." *Fast Company*.
7 De Geus, A. (1997) *The Living Company*, Nicholas Brealey Publishing, London.
8 Wacker, W. & Taylor, J. (2001) *The Visionary's Handbook*, Harper-CollinsBusiness, New York.
9 Goleman, D. (1998) *Working with Emotional Intelligence*, Blooms-bury, New York.

Organizations in Practice

Change has always been with us, although it is only comparatively recently that "change management" has been elevated to an important business concept. This section looks at issues involved in managing change as well as case studies in four organizations:

» Dell Computer Corporation;
» St Luke's advertising agency;
» Semco; and
» Nissan.

"It's easy to fall in love with how far you've come and how much you've done. It's definitely harder to see the cracks in a structure you've built yourself, but that's all the more reason to look hard and look often. Even if something seems to be working, it can be improved."

Michael Dell, CEO, Dell Computer Corporation

"The power business has over our lives is awesome. It can promote us or dump us. It can offer self-esteem or lack of dignity. It can frighten and coerce us. It can stretch our imaginations. It can destroy families and it can sponsor and build marriages."

Andy Law, chairman, St Luke's advertising agency

"No matter how good or successful you are or how clever or crafty, your business and its future are in the hands of the people you hire. To put it a bit more dramatically, the fate of your business is actually in the hands of the youngest recruit on the staff."

Akio Morita, co-founder of Sony

Change has always been with us, although it is only comparatively recently that "change management" has been elevated to an important business concept. This clearly reflects the increasingly turbulent business environment; scarcely a day goes by without a major organization "re-inventing" itself, or otherwise embarking upon a path of transformational change (whether through total quality, process redesign, downsizing or good "old fashioned" restructuring initiatives).

Over the last decade radical change programs have spread rapidly from the private sector to the public sector, voluntary bodies, charitable organizations and, inevitably, into our personal lives. It is probably not surprising, therefore, that organizations have turned their attention to the process of change itself and how best to motivate their people to make the desired level of change.

Most of us fear change. Rather than "managing" change, it is probably more correct to say that we cope with change, we adapt to it as best we can and, if we are fortunate, we turn it to our advantage. In reality, "managing" the process of change is an illusion. It suggests that we can control or limit the effects of outside events, which are, in the short term, often beyond our control. More seriously, at a deeper level, it ignores our part in creating those events in the first place. Our best organizations do not "manage" changes thrust upon them; they are instrumental in creating those changes. They recognize their place as co-creators of their destiny.

In this section, we will look at a number of organizations and how they tackled challenges facing their businesses, with varying levels of success. Each case study will be followed by a brief analysis of key lessons or insights to be drawn.

DELL COMPUTER CORPORATION

The organization

At the age of 12, Michael Dell earned $2000 from selling stamps, and by the time he was 18, he was selling customized personal computers. He started the Dell Computer Corporation in 1984 with $1000, dropping out of his biology course at Austin University in Texas. The company, under his leadership, has gone on to become one of the most successful computer businesses in the world, redefining the industry with its direct-sale approach and the customer support model it pioneered. Dell himself is a member of the board of directors of the United States Chamber of Commerce and the Computer-world/Smithsonian Awards.

The story

Dell Computer Corporation is one of the computer industry's biggest success stories. Established in 1984, Michael Dell founded his company with the unprecedented idea of bypassing the middleman and selling custom-built computers direct to end-users. His premise from the beginning was to under-promise and over-deliver – and that applied to customers, suppliers and employees alike.

Originally an "offline" business, Dell was quick to appreciate the potential of the Internet – in fact, he built an e-business before anyone had even coined the term.

Dell.com was a natural extension of the offline business. The site is customer- rather than product-focused, being aligned by customer categories, not hardware model lines. The site directs the different type of customers to a second-level page, where the relevant line of Dell products is presented.

Pursuing this customer orientation still further, Dell brings customers into the product-planning and manufacturing processes, not just the sales process, and management encourages everyone in the company to have contact with customers.

Here's how Michael Dell himself characterizes his business approach in his book *Direct from Dell*:[1]

» Think about the customer, not the competition: competitors represent your industry's past, as, over the years, collective habits become ingrained. Customers are your future, representing new opportunities, ideas, and avenues for growth.
» Work to maintain a healthy sense of urgency and crisis: this doesn't mean that you want to fabricate deadlines or keep people so stressed that they quickly burn out. Set the bar slightly higher than you normally would, so that your people can achieve aggressive goals by working smarter.
» Turn your competition's greatest strength into a weakness: much as every great athlete has an Achilles heel, so, too, do all great companies. Study the competition's "game": exploit its weakness by exposing its greatest strength.
» Be opportunistic, but also be fast: look to find opportunity, especially when it isn't readily apparent. Focusing on the customer doesn't mean that you should ignore the competition. If something that your competition did or didn't do provided you with an opportunity today, would you recognize it and be able to act on it immediately? Today a competitive win can be decided literally one day at a time. You have to act fast, be ready, then be ready to change – fast.
» Be the hunter, not the hunted: success is a dangerous thing, as we are at once invincible and vulnerable. Always strive to keep your team focused on growing the business and on winning and acquiring new business. Even though your company may be leading the market, you never want your people to act as though you are. That leads to complacency, and complacency kills. Encourage people to think, "This is good. This worked. Now how can we take what we've proven and use it to win new business?" There's a big difference

between asking that and asking, "How can we defend our existing accounts?"

Analysis

Rebecca Saunders, in her insightful book *Business the Dell Way*,[2] attributes Dell's success to ten key factors.

1 Sell direct: Dell eliminates the middleman by custom-building IBM clones and selling them directly to consumers, thereby reducing overhead costs and eliminating dealer mark-ups. This is the original marketing concept behind Dell Computer Corporation.

2 Value and manage inventory: this is a direct consequence of Dell's sell and build approach to manufacture of PCs.

3 Don't grow for growth's sake: Dell learned this the hard way. In the early 90s, Dell Computer experienced several expansion problems, including failure of a line of low-quality laptops. Growth is good, but it's controlled growth.

4 Innovate or evaporate: equally, recognize that gradual improvement to each product line reduces risk and allows you to take advantage of rapid technological developments.

5 Market innovation: Dell was the first firm to market PCs by phone but now actively encourages business via the Web. Be alert to opportunities outside of traditional distribution channels.

6 Think and act global: a young Dell Computer – and young Michael Dell – established the first of 12 international operations. He took his firm abroad almost a decade before most technology companies.

7 Don't focus on computers, focus on customers and their needs: Dell believes in going to where customers do business to understand their needs.

8 Ally with employees: hire those who can generate ideas, train people to be creative, and create an environment that allows ideas to be tested.

9 Ally with suppliers: highest quality comes from outsourcing the manufacture of parts to suppliers with most expertise, experience, and quality in producing that part.

10 Stay the course: if the formula works, don't mess with it. Dell has been called a "methodical optimizer," someone who comes up

with a good idea, recognizes it as such, then tirelessly pursues that idea, an example being the approach to "sell-and-build."

Obsessive customer focus linked to strategic savvy is clearly instrumental to Dell's success over the years, but just as important has been Michael Dell's commitment to internal organizational processes. He himself has summed this up as setting out to build a company of owners. As he puts it in *Direct from Dell*: "Creating a culture in which every person in your organization, at every level, thinks and acts like an owner means that you need to aim to connect individual performance with your company's most important objectives. For us, that means we mobilize everyone around creating the best possible customer experience and enhancing shareholder value – and we use specific quantifiable measurements of our progress towards those goals that apply to every employee's performance. A company composed of individual owners is less focused on hierarchy and who has the nicest office, and more intent on achieving their goals."

ST LUKE'S

The organization

Although formally launched on St Luke's day in October 1995 (St Luke being the patron saint of creativity and healing), the company's roots can be traced back to the early 1990s when Andy Law and David Abraham, two senior staff from the London office of the US advertising agency Chiat Day joined a team of people drawn from Chiat Day's international network that was given the task of renewing the company's sense of purpose.

At the time their proposal that Chiat Day should become an explicitly ethical advertising company was thrown out by Chiat Day's founder, Jay Chiat. Nonetheless, Law and Abraham took the opportunity to revamp the operating practices of the London office by introducing new ways of working.

All went well until 1995, when one evening Jay Chiat called Law to tell him that the whole company, including the London office, had just been sold. Law was asked to merge the London office with the operations of a rival agency. Law and Abraham, with the backing of the creative team from the London office operation, decided they would rather go it alone. Following negotiations with the new owners, Law and Abraham bought the London operation for £1 plus a share of the profits, worth £1.2 million over seven years.

The story

When they bought the company, Law and Abraham could have kept the equity and become millionaires – on paper at least. Instead, they decided to take the opportunity to create a new kind of company, one in which:

» the company's ownership reflected everyone's contribution to the business;
» the company was built on a set of relationships rather than a hierarchy; and
» open management would be used, not traditional command and control.

To achieve this model, approximately 30% of the company's shares were distributed to employees in equal portions, regardless of salary, rank, or length of service. The remaining shares were held in a trust with the aim that the trust will always have a majority.

In fact, employees play an enormous part in the company's development. This is clearly seen in the fact that St Luke's is governed by a five-person board known as the Quest. One board member is the company's lawyer. Two are senior employees and the remaining two elected by a vote of the workforce. The Quest is the company's primary decision making vehicle on employment related issues – maternity leave, sick leave, employment contracts and so on. It meets at fortnightly intervals, and any staff member can come along as an observer.

The other main decision making forum is the monthly Flag Meeting, open to all staff. Topics covered here include reviews of performance and recent work as well as future business prospects and strategic questions facing the company. The Flag Meeting tends not to put forward initiatives but it does have the power to veto a proposal from senior managers.

Finally, there is a Monday morning briefing meeting attended by all staff and chaired by a different junior member of staff each week.

St Luke's style is also reflected in the working environment. Unlike most companies where the biggest offices go to the most senior staff, St Luke's structures its office around its clients, each of whom have a themed and specially decorated "brand meeting room" dedicated to them. Most of the rest of the building is made up of shared spaces with staff working at large common tables on a "hot desking" principle. Nobody is allowed to bag a permanent spot. All resources – like computers and mobile phones – are shared.

Perhaps the most succinct way to describe the working atmosphere at St Luke's is to quote Chairman Andy Law from his book *Open Minds*[3], in which he sets out his management philosophy in a nutshell.

TEN WAYS TO CREATE A REVOLUTION IN YOUR COMPANY

1 Ask yourself what you want out of life.
2 Ask yourself what really matters to you.
3 Give all your work-clothes to Oxfam and wear what you feel is really you.
4 Talk to people (even those you don't like) about 1 and 2. You should be feeling very uncomfortable now. You may even be sick. This is normal.
5 Give up something you most need at work (desk, company car, etc.).
6 Trust everyone you meet. Keep every agreement you make. You should be feeling a little better now.
7 Undergo a group experience (anything goes, parachuting, holidaying).
8 Rewrite your business plan to align all of the above with your customers.
9 Draw a line on the office floor and invite everyone to a brave new world.
10 Share everything you do and own fairly with everyone who crosses the line. You should be feeling liberated. Soon you will have, in this order, the following: – grateful customers, inspired employees, friendly communities, money.

Analysis

What is impressive about St Luke's is its performance. This is not just an altruistic exercise in worker democracy – the formula works as can be seen from the company's business performance. St Luke's has won a string of awards and plaudits, and has enjoyed almost continual rapid growth.

The model that Abraham and Law put in place was brilliantly suited to the company's purpose. St Luke's is an ethical company that produces advertising that is about more than selling products. Clients are encouraged to take a broader view of their social role as a way of unlocking hidden brand value. It is also recognized as one of the most creative agencies in the business, something due in no small measure to the working environment and employee attitude that the company has engendered.

Charles Leadbeater has summed up the significance of St Luke's as a business model as follows:[4]

"In an industry known for the scale of its expense accounts and egos, St Luke's represents a revolutionary model of how an advertising agency should be owned and managed. Yet the relevance of the St Luke's model goes well beyond advertising. Increasingly the competitiveness of most businesses in retailing and finance, manufacturing and tourism, depends on the knowledge, ideas and creativity of the people they employ. These are their most valuable assets. Our economies are shifting away from land, machinery and raw materials as the asset base of business to knowledge, ideas and creativity. That shift will require all businesses to ask fundamental questions about how they are owned and managed, how they pay and involve their employees . . . St Luke's has developed a powerful blend of employee ownership, participatory management and a creative work culture. The lessons from St Luke's apply to any people based, service business that makes non-standard products. This new breed of company thrives because it does not have a top-heavy management hierarchy. Information and responsibility is devolved to frontline employees. Employee ownership is the "glue" that binds these loose, networked companies together. They all promote a high performance culture, in which employee ownership helps to provide a sense of membership and common purpose.

"At their most radical, this new breed of company is challenging the very idea of what a company is for and how it should be constructed. They promote the idea of companies as communities of interests, a set of relationships rather than a financial entity or a neatly bounded, organizational hierarchy.

"The new model of ownership, management and compensation that these companies are creating may not apply as well to very large companies that operate in capital intensive industries. However the factors which make this new approach so potent – the importance of innovation and creativity, the emergence of more devolved and networked forms of organization – will affect most companies in the next few years regardless of the sector they operate in."

There are issues, however. An open management style requires a lot of patience. Command and control might not be pretty but it is quick – at St Luke's everything has to be negotiated.

Continuing growth also presents its own dilemmas. Any company that grows very fast can find it a challenge to get new employees to buy into the prevailing culture.

On the other hand, whether the model developed at St Luke's has the resilience to cope with a downturn in its business fortunes (the company has enjoyed continuous growth since its creation) remains to be seen. In the meantime, St Luke's makes a compelling case study for any business leader seeking a new approach.

SEMCO

The organization

Ricardo Semler is a Brazilian industrialist who holds a majority stake in Semco, a company that manufactures marine equipment, food-service machinery, and other highly differentiated products. Most recently, Semco moved into the field of Internet services. Semler took control of the company in 1982 at the age of 24; until then, the business had been managed by his father. The company was on the brink of bankruptcy, but against a backdrop of severe recession in Brazil, Semco was transformed into a successful and globally admired business by a startling exercise in worker participation.

The story

Ricardo Semler's best selling book *Maverick*[5] chronicles the development of what has been called the world's most unusual workplace. Semco has "no receptionists, secretaries, standard hierarchies, dress codes, or executive perks;" instead it's a company "that lets you set your work hours and even your salary . . . where the standard policy is no policy."

Semler is a flamboyant, inspirational CEO, now in his late thirties who, in just ten years, transformed the company by ignoring conventional management wisdom.

At Semco, workers make corporate decisions, set their own hours, and have access to monthly financial figures. The company's management philosophy is anti-hierarchical and unorthodox, but its profits are handsome. The company operates on the basis of three key principles: work force democracy, profit sharing, and free access to information. Democracy lets employees set their own working conditions; profit sharing rewards them for doing well; information tells them how they are doing.

When the Brazilian economy took a turn downward in 1990, however, empowerment, profit sharing, self-set salaries, and other policies were no longer enough to ensure survival. The only solution was to cut permanent staff and contract out more work. But instead of contracting it to strangers, Semler gave the contracts to his own workers, setting them up in business with generous severance settlements and an offer to lease them Semco's equipment and to defer lease payments. The transition was painful but only one of the many spin-off companies set up by his workers has failed to date.

More recently, Semler has maintained his unorthodox edge by allowing his "employees" to shape the very nature of the company's business activities. According to Semler, once you say what business you're in, you put your employees into a mental straitjacket and hand them a ready-made excuse for ignoring new opportunities. So rather than dictate his company's identity, he lets his employees shape it through their individual efforts and interests. "I don't know what Semco is," he has written in a Harvard Business Review article[6] in a first-person account of his company's expansion from manufacturing to Internet services, "nor do I want to know."

Analysis

Semler has summed up some of the lessons he has learned over the years as follows.

1 Forget about the top line.
2 Never stop being a start-up.
3 Don't be a nanny (treat your employees like adults).
4 Let talent find its place.
5 Make decisions quickly and openly when it comes to reviewing proposals for new businesses.

Semler's particular genius has been to recognize the self-organizing potentials that were unleashed within Semco and how he could enable the creation of a new organization around them.

It's intriguing that Semler's personal epiphany seems to have arisen out of his sense that he was being physically destroyed by his workaholic life style. His sickness brought about a dramatic reappraisal of his work patterns – he reduced his working hours, delegated more and more, for example, and performed a complete reformulation of his approach to managing the company. In short, personal crisis was the catalyst for organizational renewal.

As time went by, Semler became more and more committed to this process, even though he didn't know where it would take him. When asked about his role in the company, he describes himself as "the questioner," "the challenger" and "the catalyst." He prides himself on the fact that he is now virtually dispensable, spending less and less time working explicitly for the company.

NISSAN

The organization

Nissan was established in 1933 to manufacture and sell small Datsun passenger cars and auto parts. These days, Nissan is engaged in corporate activities on a global scale, operating 20 manufacturing companies in 16 countries around the world with a combined annual production volume of approximately 2.6 million units and marketing Nissan vehicles in 191 countries and territories worldwide.

In March 1999, Nissan and Renault signed a comprehensive alliance agreement aimed at strengthening Nissan's financial position and at the same time achieving profitable growth for both companies.

The story

In 1999, Japanese car giant Nissan was in a bad way. So bad that when Renault, the French car company, took a 36.8% stake in Nissan, business commentators were calling the task facing Carlos Ghosn, Renault's appointment into the role of chief operating officer, mission impossible. Yet two years later, losses of 684 billion yen ($6.1 billion) had been turned into a profit of 331 billion yen. Ghosn described the transformation as the company moving from the emergency ward to the recovery room.

The Nissan story is not just an example of an impressive corporate recovery, but also a case study of how to work in an alliance, and of how a foreigner can shake up a failing Japanese company, despite a perceived cultural gulf. That said, Ghosn consistently plays down the cultural aspect: "I don't know what is a Japanese company," he has said. "As with anywhere else, you just get bad ones and great ones."

The real challenge now has been to change attitudes at Nissan, from top to bottom and from design right through to sales. One of the first things that Ghosn noticed on assuming his new role was that nobody seemed to take responsibility when things went wrong. Managers blamed the strength of the yen or the poor state of Japan's economy for the company's plight, ignoring the fact that competitors such as Honda and Toyota were prospering.

An early initiative by the new CEO was to form cross-functional teams to work on ways to break down barriers between departments. But when he outlined his recovery plan to his senior managers, there were distinct pockets of resistance; however, he began to see changes as a number of key executives agreed that the plan had merit. These days, he gives a very positive assessment of Japanese managers: "When you get a clear strategy and communicate your priorities, it's a pleasure working in Japan. The Japanese are so organized and know how to make the best of things. They respect leadership."

Analysis

Ghosn has described the challenge of managing an alliance between two very different cultures as dealing with "the contradiction between synergy and identity." Too much synergy and you lose identity. "Identity matters," he says, "because it is the basis of motivation, and motivation is the fuel that companies run on." In his view, it remains vital that Renault people identify with their company and brand, just as Nissan staff should still do with theirs.

There is a view of alliances, particularly in the car industry, that they too often achieve the opposite of synergy. Two plus two can equal three. It is to Ghosn's credit that he has avoided that sub-optimal trap.

At a broader level, the 1990s were tricky times for many Japanese businesses. Company leaders came to realize that the bursting of the bubble economy and the over-hanging recession of 1993 were more than temporary setbacks – they were signs of substantial problems with Japan's long-term competitiveness.

The heart of the crisis was steadily diminishing levels of white-collar productivity, a problem worldwide but a particularly severe one for Japanese businesses. This is a problem that Japan continues to grapple with today. In these ultra-competitive times, not even the most efficient companies can sustain the high overheads they have accumulated. As a result, according to a Harvard Business Review article[7], many companies are beginning to downsize or look for ways to trim the size of their payrolls. But restructuring will not be enough. Japanese leaders must craft a solution that combines short-term cuts with long-term innovations in generating productivity, job flexibility, and continued worker commitment.

The commitment to lifetime employment, so long a cornerstone of Japanese business practice, has become unsustainable. Guaranteed jobs for life make for a rigid job market, cash shortfalls (as in Nissan's case) which then lead to a reduction of investment in research and development, not to mention difficulties with trading partners in the international business community. There is also a danger that what is seen as worker loyalty is actually illusory, in truth amounting to not much more than worker inertia. Similarly, the Japanese company practice of training workers in specific organizational practices, rather than equipping them with transferable skills, has proved unhealthy and restrictive. Japan's economy needs more mobility and fluidity in its job market; without these qualities, the economy will contain a deep structural flaw guaranteed to extend the length of any recession, possibly by years. Japan's companies must address these issues if its post-war track record of largely unbroken economic success is to continue.

NOTES

1 Dell, M. (1999) *Direct from Dell*, HarperCollinsBusiness, New York.
2 Saunders, R. (2000) *Business the Dell Way*, Capstone, Oxford.
3 Law, A. (1998) *Open Minds*, Orion, London.
4 Leadbeater, C. (1997) "A piece of the action: employee ownership, equity pay and the knowledge economy." Demos, London.
5 Semler, R. (2001) *Maverick* (rev. ed.), Random House Business Books, New York.
6 Semler, R. "How we went digital without a strategy." Harvard Business Review, September 2000.
7 Hori, S. "Fixing Japan's white-collar economy: a personal view." Harvard Business Review, November–December 1993.

Key Concepts and Thinkers

This section contains a selective glossary of key terms, key concepts and key thinkers associated with organizational theory and practice.

Like many other business subjects, the theory and practice of what goes on in and around organizations have a language all their own. Here is a selective glossary of some of the key terms, key concepts and key thinkers associated with the subject.

Accidental career – This is what you have if your career has evolved by chance circumstances rather than through positive choice.

Activity based management – Activity based management looks at how efficiently products and services are delivered to customers by analyzing the primary business processes involved in delivering those products and services. This customer perspective breaks down the traditional functional silos since business processes are, by and large, activities that are linked *across* functional boundaries.

Adhocracy – A non-bureaucratic networked organization with a highly organic organizational design.

Ansoff, Igor – Distinguished academic and consultant, who introduced a number of key ideas including gap analysis, synergy, corporate advantage, and paralysis by analysis which helped to form the basic vocabulary of modern day strategic thinking. His first, and most influential book , *Corporate Strategy,* was published in 1962.

Balanced scorecard – Concept developed by Robert Kaplan and David Norton of the Harvard Business School, that supplements traditional financial performance measures with customer, internal business process, and innovation and learning measures.

Bricks and mortar – Companies that use traditional methods of selling and distributing products.

Business process re-design – This involves changing both organizational structure and processes to ensure that future customer needs can be anticipated and fulfilled in the most cost-effective manner. It should not be confused with crude cost-cutting exercises (such as downsizing), although many organizations have used both approaches simultaneously, with the result that the value of process redesign has been tarnished in the eyes of many managers.

Career choke – This is what happens to your career when you don't get that job that you fondly imagined was yours, say when your boss moves on.

Chandler, Alfred – Born in 1918, Chandler is a Pulitzer Prize-winning business historian who was very influential in shaping organizations thinking about strategy in the 1960s and 1970s. He was the first person to make explicit the link between strategy and structure.

Clusters – Critical masses of linked industries in one place that enjoy a high level of success in their particular field. Famous examples are Silicon Valley and Hollywood, but clusters can be found everywhere.

Communities of practice – Groups that form within an organization, typically of their own accord, where members are drawn to one other by a common set of needs that may be both professional and social. Compared to project teams, communities of practice are voluntary, longer-lived, have no specific deliverable, and are responsible only to themselves. Because they are free of formal structures and hierarchy within an organization, they can be viewed as subversive.

Competitive intelligence – In a world of rapid technological change where new and sometimes surprising competitors can suddenly appear, a company's success will increasingly depend on how effectively it can gather, analyze and use information. According to Larry Kahaner, author of competitive intelligence, companies that can turn raw information into powerful intelligence will "build market share, launch new products, increase profits and destroy competitors."

Core competencies – The key strengths of an organization (sometimes called distinctive capabilities). Gary Hamel and C.K. Prahalad, authors of *Competing for the Future*, define core competencies as "a bundle of skills and technologies (rather than a simple or discrete skill or technology) that enables the company to provide a particular benefit to customers."

Core competents – The small number of people in an organization who are absolutely vital to that organization's success. Bill Gates has reflected that if 20 people were to leave Microsoft, the company would risk bankruptcy. In a study by the Corporate Leadership Council, a computer firm recognized 100 "core competents" out of 16,000 employees; a software company had 10 out of 11,000; and a transportation group deemed 20 of its 33,000 as really critical.

Corporate culture – Is the pattern of basic assumptions that a given group has invented, discovered, or developed in learning to cope with its problems of external adaptation and internal integration, and that have worked well enough to be considered valid, and therefore taught to new members as the correct way to perceive, think and feel in relation to those problems.

Corporate strategy – Concerned with mission and vision, portfolio management, acquisitions and divestments. Generic corporate strategies include growth, portfolio extension, care taking, harvesting or retrenchment.

Creepback – A tendency for former staff to be re-hired on the quiet after over-enthusiastic sackings have been made.

Critical success factors – The key organizational capabilities that differentiate competitors in industry by their ability to meet customer needs.

Cultural diagnostics – Cultural diagnosis is a vital part of the strategic process because it allows us to become aware of the filters that we use to process our experience, both as individuals and as members of organizations, and the degree of "selectivity" that is involved in interpreting those experiences. It is a complex area, not least because it deals directly with the foibles that we have as human beings.

Customer intimacy – Building customer loyalty in the long term by continually tailoring and shaping products and services to the needs of an increasingly choosy customer. Organizations pursuing this strategy frequently try to build lifetime relationships with their customers.

Customer relationship management (CRM) – A set of techniques and approaches designed to provide personalized service to customers and to increase customer loyalty. Increasingly viewed as a strategic issue, and one that typically requires technological support.

Customer sacrifice – The gap between what customers settle for and what they really want. Successful companies reduce customer sacrifice by cultivating learning relationships. The more customers "teach" the company, the better it can provide just what they want and the more difficult it becomes for competitors, to whom customers would have to teach their preferences afresh, to lure them away.

Desk rage – Long hours and the growing pressures of the workplace are leading to increasing outbreaks of office strife or "desk rage." As stress builds in the office, workers are increasingly venting their frustrations on colleagues.

Differentiation – The ability to be unique in the industry along some dimensions valued by the customer. For example, this might be through product or service leadership or through understanding and knowing customers better than competitors.

Discontinuities – One-off changes in the marketplace that force radical organizational change.

Disintermediation – Buzzword for how the Internet is cutting out the middlemen, enabling wholesalers/manufacturers to sell direct to the end user. Classic potential victims of disintermediation are estate agents and travel agents.

Distinctive capabilities – See *core competencies*.

Downshifting – The deliberate decision by somebody to simplify their life by, for example, balancing work and home life, or reducing levels of financial commitment, at the expense of income.

Downsizing – Restructuring an organization in a declining market where the level of resources (manpower, support functions etc.) are inappropriate to meeting current customer needs.

Drucker, Peter – When Peter Drucker wrote *The Concept of the Corporation* in 1945, he could find only two firms that offered their staff management training and only three academic courses in the subject. Since then, of course, the management business has boomed, and Drucker has gone on to become, in the words of *The Economist,* "the greatest thinker management theory has produced." Opinion has long been divided about Drucker. Now in his nineties, he still commands more respect than affection in some quarters and even that respect is tempered by a sense that his work lacks academic credibility. Interestingly, it is in the community of practicing managers where Drucker's reputation has largely been built. Perhaps that is because he has always written from the standpoint that the world of work is essentially about human endeavor.

E-business – Using the Internet or other electronic means to conduct business. The two most common models are B2C (business to consumer) and B2B (business to business). Partly due to news coverage given to high profile companies like Amazon, B2C is the better known model; on the other hand, B2B probably has more long-term potential than its more glamorous cousin.

E-commerce – Commercial activity conducted via the Internet.

E-lancers – Independent contractors connected through personal computers and electronic networks. These electronically connected freelancers join together into fluid and temporary networks to produce and sell goods and services.

External positioning – The relationship of the organization with the external world in terms of its markets, customers and the broader environment.

Fayol, Henry – Perhaps more than anybody, Fayol (1841–1925), a mining engineer and manager by profession, defined the nature and working patterns of the twentieth century organization. In his book, *General and Industrial Management*, published in 1916, Fayol laid down 14 principles of management (see Chapter 3 for more details). Fayol also characterized the activities of a commercial organization into six basic elements: technical; commercial; financial; security; accounting; and management. The management function, Fayol believed, consisted of planning, organizing, commanding, coordinating and controlling. Many practicing managers today would probably identify similar elements as the core of their activities.

Focus – A concept popularized by Michael Porter to describe companies that select a market segment or group of segments within an industry and serve customers in these segments to the exclusion of others.

Gap analysis – A method for exploring the gap between current reality and the vision of the organization, both in terms of external customer needs and internal capabilities.

Globalization – The integration of economic activity across national or regional boundaries, a process that has been accelerated by the impact of information technology.

Handy, Charles – Writer, lecturer, broadcaster, and self-styled social philosopher. In his book *The Age of Unreason* (Hutchinson, London, 1989), he explored a number of organizational forms that he expected to emerge during the 1990s and beyond. These included the following.

1   The shamrock organization: a form of organization based around a core of essential executives and workers supported by outside contractors and part-time help.
2   The federal organization: a form of decentralized set-up in which the center's powers are given to it by the outlying groups; the center therefore co-ordinates, advises, influences and suggests rather than directs or controls. Federalism, says Handy, is the way to combine the autonomy of individual parts with the economics of co-ordination.
3   The triple I organization: the three "I's" are information, intelligence and ideas. This type of organization, says Handy, will resemble a university and will seek to make "added value out of knowledge." To achieve this end, this type of organization "increasingly uses smart machines, with smart people to work with them."

Not only was Handy remarkably prescient in anticipating the growth of outsourcing, telecommuting, the intellectual capital movement, and the rise of knowledge workers *inter alia*, he also foresaw how these developments might impact on the individual. It was his concept of the portfolio worker that arguably provided a way forward for that part of the whole downshifting movement of the nineties.

Herzberg, Frederick – In his book *Motivation to Work* (John Wiley, 1959), Herzberg coined the terms hygiene factors and motivational factors as a basis for exploring what motivated people to work well and happily.

Informate – Term coined by Harvard academic Shoshana Zuboff to describe the capacity for information technology to translate and make visible organizational processes, objects, behaviors, and events.

Innovation – A significant change or improvement in the products or services of an organization or the process by which they are produced.

Intellectual capital – Intellectual material: knowledge, information, intellectual property, experience; that can be put to use to create wealth. In a business context, the sum total of what employees in an organization know that gives it a competitive edge.

Internal capabilities or competencies – What the organization is good at. Something an organization can do that its potential competitors cannot.

Internal constraints – Factors that can inhibit an organization's ability to achieve desired outcomes. These factors include the level of resources available, knowledge of new markets and products, the cultural adaptability of the organization to new opportunities etc.

Intranet – A network designed to organize and share information that is accessible only by a specified group or organization.

Jaques, Elliott – For over 50 years, Jaques has consistently advocated the need for a scientific approach to understanding work systems. He argues that there is a "widespread, almost universal, underestimation of the impact of organization on how we go about our business." He believes, for example, that rapid change in people's behavior is achieved less through altering their psychological make-up and more by revising organizational structures and managerial leading practices. His book *Requisite Organization* challenges many current assumptions about effective organizations, particularly in the field of hierarchy of which Jaques is a fan. Some find his theories indigestible, but for those who persist there is a wealth of challenging material that undermines much conventional organizational wisdom.

Key performance indicators – Key performance indicators (KPI) are normally combined as a basket of measures to cover all critical areas of the organization. KPI's are generally selected from the following categories of information: customer satisfaction; product and service innovation; operational improvement; employee morale and commitment; financial health; and cultural diagnosis.

Killer app – A new good or service that, by being first in the market place, dominates it, often returning several hundred percent on the initial investment.

Knowledge management – A system, most often computer-based, used to share information in a company with the goal of increasing levels of responsiveness and innovation.

Learning organization – Peter Senge characterizes learning organizations as places where "people continually expand their capacity to create the results they truly desire, where new and expansive patterns of thinking are nurtured, where collective aspiration is set free, and where people are continually learning how to learn together.'' He also acknowledges that the idea of a learning organization is a vision.

Maslow, Abraham - Abraham Maslow remains one of the most widely known experts on human behavior and motivation. His psychological perspectives on management, such as the hierarchy of needs, are still studied today in business schools all over the world. Maslow's most influential business book, *Eupsychian Management*, is a stimulating but not always easy read that demonstrates clearly why Maslow was an unparalleled thinker and innovator in applying human behavior to the workplace.

Mass customization - The cost-efficient mass production as a matter of routine of goods and services in lot sizes of one or just a few at a time.

Micro-careers - With the death of the job for life went the notion of getting paid to do broadly the same thing throughout your working days. Micro-careers are those distinct and separate chunks of activity that will characterize an individual's working life in the twenty-first century.

Mintzberg, Henry - A member of McGill University's Faculty of Management since 1968, has written extensively about the process of strategy formation, and the design of organizations. His well-known books include *The Nature of Managerial Work* (1973), *The Structuring of Organizations* (1979), *Power In and Around Organizations* (1983), and *Mintzberg on Management: Inside Our Strange World of Organizations* (1989). His book, *The Rise and Fall of Strategic Planning*, won the best book award of the Academy of Management in 1995.

Mission - In theory, mission statements should capture the essence of the organization, those things about it which are truly unique and provide the platform from which the organization can create the future. Management writers sometimes refer to this as establishing purpose or strategic intent. The statement takes the form of a formal declaration of what an organization is all about rooted in a clear understanding of reality. In practical terms, mission statements rarely live up to very much and are often little more than a collection of management buzzwords that are not rooted in organizational reality.

New capitalism – According to Robert Reich, former US Secretary for Labor, "Old capitalism's giant companies had vast numbers of employees; new capitalism's giant companies have few employees. The issues of old capitalism law on property, contract, limited liability, tort, bankruptcy, all of these are no longer really appropriate. The key assets of new capitalism are not defined as physical property but as intellectual assets, many embedded in people."

One-to-one marketing – Customizing and personalizing a product or service to meet an individual's specific needs

Operational excellence – Providing customers with reliable products or services at competitive prices and delivered with minimal difficulty or inconvenience. The object of the organization adopting this strategy is to lead its industry in price and convenience.

Organizational behavior (OB) – The study of human behavior, attitudes and performance within an organizational setting. OB draws on theory, methods and principles from such disciplines as psychology, sociology, and cultural anthropology to learn about individual perception, values, learning capabilities, and actions while working with groups and within the total organization. OB also can involve analyzing the external environment's effect on the organization and its learning resources, missions, objectives, and strategies.

Organization development (OD) – According to Richard Beckhard, writing in his book *Organization Development: Strategies and Models* (Addison-Wesley, 1969), "OD is an effort that is (1) planned, (2) organization-wide, and (3) managed from the top, to increase (4) organizational effectiveness and health, through (5) planned interventions in the organization's "processes," using behavioral-science knowledge."

Out of the garage – A term for a young company that has just moved to its first real office.

Paradigm – A constellation of concepts, values, perceptions and practices shared by a community which form a particular vision of reality and collective mood that is the basis of the way that the community organizes itself.

Pascale, Richard – Born in 1938, Richard Pascale was a member of the faculty of Stanford's Graduate School of Business for 20 years. Now a leading business consultant, he has written or co-authored three highly challenging books: *The Art of Japanese Management* (1981), *Managing on the Edge* (1990), and *Surfing on the Edge of Chaos* (2000).

Peters, Tom – Former McKinsey consultant and co-author (with Bob Waterman) of *In Search of Excellence* (Harper & Row, 1982), the most popular management book of recent times with sales of over six million globally.

Portfolio working – Coined by Charles Handy, portfolio working is a way of describing how the different bits of work in our life fit together to form a balanced whole. There are five main categories of work for the portfolio: *wage work* and *fee work*, which are both forms of paid work; *homework, gift work,* and *study work,* which are all free work.

Product leadership – An organization achieves this by creating a continuous stream of state of the art products and services.

Product overlap – This occurs when more than one generation of the same product is available simultaneously. The original version of a piece of software may sell at a reduced price alongside the latest version at a higher price.

PYMWYMIC – A company that acts according to its values and beliefs, as in a "put your money where your mouth is company."

Reality check – A reality check is any tool, technique, method or device used by an individual or organization to provide feedback on their place in the world. Reality checks include tools and techniques that are recognized as "strategic" (such as industry analysis, competitor analysis and so on) and many others that are not (customer research, employee feedback or merely reading trade magazines).

Re-purposing – Originally coined by US TV executives to describe the process of "freshening up" a new series of a well established TV series whose popularity is flagging by introducing new characters and plot-lines. The term is now being adopted by companies seeking to re-establish forward momentum.

Scenario planning – A tool pioneered by Shell in the 1970s that involves identifying and planning for a range of possible futures. The idea, in a nutshell, is to improve a company's capacity to respond to whichever future comes to pass.

Schein, Edgar – Born in 1928, and a professor at the MIT Sloan School of Management, Edgar H Schein is sometimes seen as the "inventor" of the idea of corporate culture. More recently, his work has explored the nature of the psychological contract between employer and employee, and also career anchors – the idea that we each have an underlying career value that we are unwilling to give up.

Scientific management – An approach to work devised around a century ago by Frederick Taylor that involved detailed observation and measurement of even the most routine work to find the optimum mode of performance. Taylor advocated the use of time-and-motion study as a means of analyzing and standardizing work activities.

Seven S model – Widely used analytical tool, devised by Richard Pascale and Anthony Athos, that evaluates organizations under seven key headings to which managers need to pay attention. The seven are: strategy, structure, systems, skills, style, shared values, and staff. Some of these areas are "hard" (i.e. strategy, structure, and systems) and some are "soft" (style, staff, and shared values). "Skills" is placed centerpiece because it is both "hard" and "soft," comprising both the distinctive capabilities of key personnel and the core competencies of the organization as a whole.

Shared vision – In a corporation, a shared vision changes people's relationship with the company. It is no longer "their company;" it becomes "our company." A shared vision is the first step in allowing people who mistrusted each other to begin to work together. It creates a common identity.

SOHO – Small office, home office a term used to describe what in North America is currently the fastest growing category of employment, namely the rise of self-employment and home-based businesses.

Strategic inflection points – A term coined by Andy Grove to describe a moment in the life of a business, when its fundamentals are about to change for better or worse.

Taylor, Frederick W. – The world's first efficiency expert and "the father of scientific management." Taylor's work with car-making legend Henry Ford led directly to the mass production techniques that created 15 million Model Ts between 1910 and 1927, and that set the pattern for industrial working practice world-wide. Although he lived through little of it – he died in 1915 – Taylor's influence on the twentieth century is unquestionable. Peter Drucker, for example, rates him alongside Freud and Darwin as a maker of the modern world. And despite its critics, Taylorism and the production methods that it spawned in the early part of the twentieth century, lives on, whether in the form of re-engineering (a direct descendant of scientific management), the continuing debate about the de-skilling of many jobs, or the standardized global practices of companies like McDonald's.

Technology adoption life cycle – Model created by Geoffrey A. Moore to demonstrate the various points at which individuals will become involved with a technological innovation. Moore identifies five key groups that will become involved with any new technology at various stages of its life cycle:

1 Innovators - the technology enthusiasts
2 Early adopters - the visionaries
3 Early majority - the pragmatists
5 Late majority - the conservatives
6 Laggards - the skeptics

Ten X force – Term used by Intel CEO Andy Grove to describe a super-competitive force that threatens the future of a business.

Transformation – A one-time, discontinuous shift in financial performance, industry benchmarks (e.g. cycle time, quality, costs), or climate. An indicator of transformation is when employees say theirs is a different organization to the one it was five years ago.

Unique selling proposition (USP) – Best defined as a company's unique point of difference, the USP of an organization is the unique way in which it matches its internal capabilities with external market opportunities in order to gain competitive advantage.

Value added – In essence, the difference between the value of a firm's output and the cost of the firm's inputs.

Virtual organization – An organizational form that consists of a loose (and often temporary) combination of technology, expertise and networks.

Vision – A company's view of its future that is compelling and stretching, but that is also viewed as achievable. A corporate vision for the future has to be grounded in awareness. If not, it quickly becomes a wish-driven strategy meritorious in all respects except for the fact that it will never be achieved.

Weber, Max – Weber (1864–1920) was a German University professor who was the first person to describe organizations as having the qualities of a machine, a metaphor that persisted throughout the twentieth century. Weber is sometimes described, unfairly, as the father of bureaucracy.

Resources

Countless words have been written about what goes on in and around organizations. This chapter identifies some of the best resources around, including books, articles, journals, magazines, and Websites.

ANNOTATED BIBLIOGRAPHY

Over the years, literally thousands of books have been published about organizations. Here is a list of some of the best.

Adams S. (1996) *The Dilbert Principle*, HarperBusiness, New York

Not since the early days of *The Far Side* by Gary Larson has there been a cartoon strip to match Dilbert, a mouthless bespectacled computer nerd whose observations on modern business life are poignant, irreverent, and painfully funny. For workers around the world, Dilbert has become an essential part of their lives, a touchstone with reality when the world around them seems to be going crazy, and a mouthpiece for their unvoiced concerns and feelings. If you are not familiar with the work of Scott Adams, sample one of the Dilbert anthologies (*Build a Better Life By Stealing Office Supplies* is a very good starting point) and you will soon be smitten.

Baldock R. (2000) *The Last Days of the Giants?* John Wiley, New York

This book looks at what the corporate giants of the twentieth century need to do to survive in the twenty-first. According to Baldock, big firms are going to have to radically alter the way they do things. His prescription for survival involves three stages: first companies should re-assess the economics of sales and delivery channels, secondly they should move to a more customer-centric business model, and finally they must turn their business model through 180 degrees in order to come up with value-creating packages that satisfy consumer intentions.

Brown S.L. and Eisenhardt K.M. (1998) *Competing on the Edge: Strategy as Structured Chaos*, Harvard Business School Press, Boston, MA

Competing on the Edge was one of the first (and remains one of the best) books to translate leading-edge complexity concepts from science into management practice. For those readers who are not familiar with complexity theory, the edge of chaos is a key concept which suggests that systems that exist at the boundary zone between chaos and stability are most capable of evolving to meet (continually) emerging new orders. The authors use a wealth of case studies and interviews to illustrate the practical implications of this for business today.

Burton-Jones A. (1998) *Knowledge Capitalism*, Oxford University Press, Oxford

Burton-Jones marshals an impressive range of evidence in this closely argued exploration of how the shift to a knowledge-based economy is redefining the shape and nature of organizations. He also describes the emergence of a new breed of capitalist, one dependent on knowledge rather than physical resources. There are plenty of easier reads about the knowledge economy on the market, but those looking for substance rather than eye-catching glibness will be pleased to find in *Knowledge Capitalism* a book that provides frequent moments of insight without compromising *gravitas*.

Christensen C.M. (1997) *Innovator's Dilemma: When New Technologies Cause Great Firms to Fail*, Harvard Business School Press, Boston, MA

According to Christensen, great companies can fail because, paradoxically, they do everything right. His book demonstrates why outstanding companies lose their market leadership when confronted with disruptive technology, and suggests how others can avoid a similar fate. He cites examples from, amongst others, computer disk drive manufacturers, discount retailing, pharmaceuticals, and the automobile industry.

Davis S. & Meyer C. (1998) *Blur: The Speed of Change in the Connected Economy*, Addison-Wesley, Reading, MA

The authors, who are both based at the Ernst & Young Center for Business Innovation in Boston, maintain that "connectivity, speed, and the growth of intangible value" have catapulted business into a period of unprecedented transition that demands immediate and creative attention. Citing examples including Amazon.com, singer David Bowie, and the Beanie Baby toy phenomenon, they show how a willingness to step away from conventional thinking is crucial for continued success.

De Geus A. (1997) *The Living Company*, Nicholas Brealey, London

Drawing on unpublished research conducted by Shell in the early 1980s, Arie de Geus – the man widely credited for originating the concept of the "learning organization" – believes that most companies fail because they focus too narrowly on financial performance and pay insufficient attention to themselves as communities of human beings with the potential to learn, adapt and grow. The living company, he says, emphasizes knowledge rather than capital, and adaptability rather than core competencies. De Geus won the Edwin G. Booz prize for Most Insightful Management Book back in 1997 and so it is a little disappointing that his ideas have not yet broken through into the mainstream. Nonetheless, anybody with an interest in organizational learning will find something of value here.

Dyson J. (1997) *Against the Odds, An Autobiography*, Orion Business Books, London

Once rejected by the likes of Hoover and Electrolux, James Dyson's machine has literally "cleaned up" and made its inventor a multimillion-aire. In this book, Dyson describes his early years at the Royal College of Art, his initial successes with the Ballbarrow (a tough, stable plastic wheelbarrow with a large red plastic ball instead of a wheel), through the years spent perfecting the design of the dual cyclone and the battle to have it manufactured. More autobiography than business book, there is nonetheless plenty to be gleaned here about Dyson's management methods, particularly in a chapter entitled "A New Philosophy of Business."

Gardner H. (1996) *Leading Minds – An Anatomy of Leadership*, HarperCollins, New York

Gardner takes a variety of well-known leaders – as diverse as Margaret Thatcher and Gandhi – and tries to tease out what it is that made them so successful. He tops and tails his book with chapters on his theoretical framework and sandwiches the biographies in the middle. Gardner demonstrates brilliantly the qualities and experience needed by "leading minds," although less helpfully offers no practical guidance as to how readers might develop their own leadership skills.

Goldsmith W. & Clutterbuck D. (1997) *The Winning Streak Mark II*, Orion Business Books, London

In this follow-up to their 1984 bestseller, Goldsmith and Clutterbuck continue their research into how some organizations have managed to achieve sustained excellent performance. The authors identify 25 top companies from around the world – including Granada, Rentokil, Reuters and Vodafone – and investigate their management strategy. They also look at the lessons to be learned from companies who have not maintained their competitive edge.

Handy C. (2001) *The Elephant and the Flea*, Hutchinson, London

In his latest book (and his best for some time), self-styled social philosopher Handy explores the business world of the twenty-first century which he claims "will be a world of fleas and elephants, of large conglomerates and small individual entities, of large political and economic blocs and small countries." The smart thing, it seems, is to be the flea on the back of the elephant because a flea can be global as easily as one of the elephants but can more easily be swept away. Elephants are a guarantee of continuity but fleas provide the innovation. A fascinating premise, outlined lucidly by Handy in one of the first "must-reads" of this century.

Heller R. (1997) *In Search of European Excellence*, HarperCollins, London

With a nod to the Peters and Waterman classic, Robert Heller sets out to identify the key strategies with which Europe's most successful companies are beating their competition. When he looked at the state of European business, he found that Europe's old reactionaries are still in the majority, but that their ascendancy is rapidly draining away.

Heller gives convincing examples of European companies that have made wholehearted efforts to change. As ever with a book that draws on a large number of case studies, one or two of the companies praised have slipped from grace in recent times. This does not undermine Heller's basic thesis but it does demonstrate how tough it is to hold onto industry leadership once attained.

Jaques E. (1996) *Requisite Organization*, Cason Hall, Gloucester, MA

Based on Jaques' latest research, this is a thorough revision of the original book published in 1989. *Requisite Organization* challenges many current assumptions about effective organizations, particularly in the field of hierarchy – of which Jaques is a fan. Some may find his theories indigestible, but for those who persist there is a wealth of challenging material that undermines much conventional organizational wisdom.

Kanigel R. (1997) *The One Best Way*, Little Brown, New York

The One Best Way is an illuminating biography of Frederick W. Taylor, the efficiency expert and "the father of scientific management." Although he lived through little of it – he died in 1915, aged 59 – Taylor's influence on the twentieth century is unquestionable. Peter Drucker, for example, rates him alongside Freud and Darwin as a maker of the modern world. And despite its critics, Taylorism lives on, whether in the form of re-engineering (a direct descendant of scientific management), the continuing debate about the de-skilling of jobs, or the global standardization of companies like McDonald's. At 570 pages, the book is definitely top-heavy with detail. However, as an introduction to arguably the world's first management consultant, it makes fascinating reading.

Kaplan R.S. & Norton D.P. (1996) *The Balanced Scorecard*, Harvard Business School Press, Boston, MA

Many management writers have written in general terms on the limitations of relying on traditional financial measures to assess business performance. But by setting out with the aim of building a comprehensive framework of broadly based performance measures that provides a process for organizations to link long-term strategic objectives with short-term actions, Kaplan and Norton have taken performance measurement to the heart of organizational success in the long term. The authors demonstrate how to use measures in four categories – financial performance, customer knowledge, internal business processes, and learning and growth – to build a robust system that aligns individual, organizational, and cross-departmental initiatives.

Katzenbach J. and Smith D. (1993) *The Wisdom of Teams*, Harvard Business School Press, Boston, MA

According to Katzenbach and Smith – two senior McKinsey consultants – teams are "the primary building blocks of company performance." For this book, the authors talked with hundreds of people in more than 50 teams from 30 companies in a bid to discover what differentiates various levels of team performance, where and how teams work best, and how generally to enhance team effectiveness. Some of their findings are common sense – e.g. teams with a genuine commitment to performance goals and to a common purpose outperform those who place a greater emphasis on teambuilding. Others are at face value surprising (formal hierarchy, they say, is actually good for teams). In a chapter towards the end of the book they describe how top management can usefully support the development of a team-based culture.

Law A. (1998) *Open Minds*, Orion, London

St Luke's is a high-profile London-based advertising agency and Andy Law has been the company's iconoclastic chairman since 1995. Owned entirely by its employees, all physical resources – offices, PCs etc. – in the company are shared, and there is little hierarchy. Employees are involved in almost all decisions, including setting their own pay rises. Whether the model developed at St Luke's has the resilience to cope with a down-turn in its business fortunes (the company has enjoyed continuous growth since its creation) remains to be seen. In the meantime, *Open Minds* makes a compelling case study, describing and explaining as it does the business practices and philosophy behind this fascinating company.

Lewis J. (1999) *Trusted Partners*, Free Press, New York

Mergers and alliances on an ever-grander scale are a feature of the global economy. *Trusted Partners* describes how to build trust between organizations that are forging alliances of various types with other companies, and explores how interpersonal relationships are a critical element of that. Lewis goes well beyond theoretical analysis of the nature of trust between corporate "rivals" to lay out some practical and eminently sensible steps involved in building and maintaining trust.

Lewis M. (2001) *Next: The Future Just Happened*, Norton, New York

In which Michael Lewis, author of the best seller *The New New Thing* sets out to restore the Internet's tarnished reputation as a tool of revolution. Highly readable, as usual, Lewis presents the Internet as a powerful weapon for toppling the established organizational powers-that-be.

Moore J.F. (1996) *The Death of Competition*, HarperCollins, New York

Business as ecosystem – Moore explores the biological metaphor in great detail and with considerable insight. One of the first and arguably the best exploration of leadership and strategy in a future that Moore envisions will be characterized by organized chaos.

Peters T. & Waterman R. (1982) *In Search of Excellence*, Warner Books, New York

With the publication of *In Search of Excellence* nearly 20 years ago, Tom Peters and co-author Bob Waterman changed the way organizations thought about themselves. Notions of embracing a paradoxical world of constant change, of providing exemplary customer service, and of the need for high-speed response are now mainstream corporate thinking, but during the mid-1980s, the challenge laid down by Peters and Waterman was enormous.

Pink D. (2001) *Free Agent Nation: How America's New Independent Workers Are Transforming The Way We Live*, Warner Books, New York

Daniel Pink looks at the seismic changes occurring in the American workforce. He highlights the shift from "organization man" to "free agent worker." Pink defines free agents as "free from the bonds of a large institution, and agents of their own futures . . . the new archetypes of work in America." A classic in the making.

Porter M. (1980) *Competitive Strategy*, Free Press, New York

What forces drive competition in an industry? How can a company be best placed to compete in the long run? Porter's book, radical in its day, was one of the first to look the whole field of competitive strategy. His work has entered the management mainstream and his techniques for analyzing industries and competitors are now widely used. For anybody wishing to increase their awareness of the industry or competitive context that they work in, Porter's models and techniques remain valid and easy to use.

Ridderstråle J. & Nordström K. (2000) *Funky Business: Talent Makes Capital Dance*, Financial Times/Prentice Hall, London

On the face of it, a business book by two Swedish professors about how successful companies differ from their competitors doesn't sound like the most riveting of reads. But *Funky Business* is no dry theoretical tome; and authors Ridderstråle and Nordström are not your standard issue academics. Unless, that is, it's normal for Swedish business professors to shave their heads, wear leather trousers, describe themselves as funksters, and call their public appearances gigs rather than seminars. Funky management, for Nordström and Ridderstråle, means innovation, constant change and, especially, reliance on people as the main source of "sustainable uniqueness." This book draws extensively from rigorously researched data but presents its findings with wit and intelligence reinforced with excellent examples.

Schwartz P. (1991) *The Art of the Long View*, John Wiley, Chichester

When it originally appeared this book was one of the first books to explain and generally demystify the scenario planning techniques developed at Royal Dutch/Shell in the 1970s. It remains probably the best, and certainly the most readily intelligible introduction to the subject.

Schwartz P. & Gibb B. (1999) *When Good Companies Do Bad Things*, John Wiley, Chichester

The authors discuss business ethics at companies such as Nestle, Texaco, Union Carbide, Nike, and Royal Dutch/Shell. They examine incidents involving each of these companies, and suggest alternative approaches to the actual damage control methods adopted by the organizations in question when they were faced with (often highly public) challenges to their reputations.

Senge P. (1990) *The Fifth Discipline*, Business Books, New York

Senge's book was one of the first to popularize the concept of the learning organization. His five core disciplines that underpin the building of a learning community are: personal mastery, mental models (the filters through which we view the world), shared vision, team learning, and systems thinking. The last of these, which Senge terms the cornerstone discipline, is covered in 70 pages in a section that represents an excellent generalist introduction to the main concepts of systems thinking, a core skill in a globalized, networked economy.

Stewart T.A. (1997) *Intellectual Capital: The New Wealth of Organizations*, Bantam Books, New York

This book has proved itself in the market place as the definitive guide to understanding and managing intangible assets. The author provides a framework, practical guide and theory of the significance of intellectual capital (defined by Stewart as "packaged useful knowledge") which is a delight to read. In an age of lightweight books on the new information age, this book is a heavyweight that explains why intellectual capital will be the foundation of corporate success in the new century.

ARTICLES (MOST RECENT FIRST)

» "Good to great." *Fast Company*, October (2001) Start with 1435 good companies. Examine their performance over 40 years. Find the 11 companies that became great. Now, here's how you can do it too.

» Hammer, M. "The superefficient company." *Harvard Business Review*, September (2001). Most companies do a great job promoting efficiency within their own walls, streamlining internal processes wherever possible. But, says Hammer, they have less success coordinating cross-company business interactions.

» "A scary Swiss meltdown." *The Economist*, July 21, (2001). How a dud strategy brought a solid company to the brink of bankruptcy.

» John S.B. & Duguid P. "Creativity versus structure: a useful tension." *Sloan Management Review*, Summer (2000). Great new ideas help only those organizations with the discipline and infrastructure needed to implement them.

» Willcocks, L.P. & Plant, R. "Pathways to e-business leadership: getting from bricks to clicks." *Sloan Management Review*, Spring (2001).

» "Change is sweet." *Fast Company*, June (2001). When is a net strategy more than just a net strategy?

» "Over the counter e-commerce." *The Economist*, May 26, 2001.

» "While Welch waited." *The Economist*, May 19, 2001. First in a series of case studies of how big established companies are developing their e-business strategies.

» Pink, D.H. "Land of the free." *Fast Company*, May (2001).

» Bonabeau E. & Meyer C. "Swarm intelligence: a whole new way to think about business." *Harvard Business Review*, May 2001.

» Webber, A.M. "How business is a lot like life." *Fast Company*, April (2001). According to Richard Pascale, if you want your company to stay alive, then try running it like a living organism. The first rule of life is also the first rule of business: adapt or die.

» Hansen, M. T. & Von Oetinger, B. "Introducing t-shaped managers: knowledge management's next generation." *Harvard Business Review*, March (2001). Most companies do a poor job of capitalizing on the wealth of expertise scattered across their organizations. The authors put forward something they call t-shaped management, which requires executives to share knowledge freely across their organization (the horizontal part of the "t"), while remaining committed to their individual business unit's performance (the vertical part).

» Kanter, M. S. "The ten deadly mistakes of wanna-dots." *Harvard Business Review*, January (2001).

» Coutu, D.L "Creating the most frightening company on earth: an interview with Andy Law of St. Luke's." *Harvard Business Review*, September–October 2000.

» Fulmer, R.M., Gibbs, P.A. & Goldsmith, M. "Developing leaders: how winning companies keep on winning." *Sloan Management Review*, Fall (2000).

» Mintzberg, H. & Van der Heyden, L. "Organigraphs: drawing how companies really work." *Harvard Business Review*, September–October (1999).

» "The rise of the infomediary." *The Economist*, Jun 26, (1999). The Internet is producing a string of racy new business models.

» "A price on the priceless." *The Economist*, Jun 26, (1999). Companies know that their competitive advantage lies increasingly in knowledge and ideas. But what are the ideas worth?

» Lovins, A.B., Lovins L.H. & Hawken, P. "A road map for natural capitalism." *Harvard Business Review,* May–June (1999).

» Hagel III, J. & Singer, M. "Unbundling the corporation." *Harvard Business Review,* March–April (1999).

» Nicholson, N. "How hardwired is human behavior." *Harvard Business Review,* July–August (1998).

» Pine II, B.J. & Gilmore, J.H. "Welcome to the experience economy." *Harvard Business Review,* July–August 1998.

» Collins J.C & Porras, J.I. "Building your company's vision." *Harvard Business Review,* September–October 1996.

» Kotter, J.P. "Leading change: why transformation efforts fail." *Harvard Business Review,* March–April (1995).

» "The vision thing." *The Economist*, September (1994).
» Kaplan R.S & Norton, D.P. "Putting the balanced scorecard to work," *Harvard Business Review,* September–October (1993).
» Treacy, M & Wiersema, F. "Customer intimacy and other value disciplines" *Harvard Business Review,* January–February (1993).
» Stayer, R. "How I learned to let my workers lead," *Harvard Business Review,* November–December (1990).

JOURNALS, MAGAZINES AND WEBSITES

For readers wanting to keep up to date with developments in the strategy field, the following list of publications and Websites are worth dipping into on a regular basis.

Business Intelligence

Publishers of some solid but very expensive reports (typically around £600 a copy). Website carries some useful free material though. www.business-intelligence.co.uk

Center for Business Innovation

Site managed by consultants Ernst and Young – quality of content varies but occasionally provokes thought. www.businessinnovation.ey.com

Company information

More and more companies are creating Websites, and the amount of information on them varies enormously, but it is always worth while looking at them, even if to rule them out as a source of information. Information on products, internal vacancies and press releases feature on many, as well as shareholder information. Press releases can often make interesting reading, as you may have read the headline story in the press but the release is likely to be more detailed, and may help give you a lead in who to approach within the firm or give you the background you need for an interview, particularly if the company is starting a new product/venture/department. In the first instance, for UK companies, try www.companyname.co.uk; for US companies, try www.companyname.com.

Companies House

A good resource to check out if you are considering setting up a limited company. Plenty of information as well as downloadable copies of the relevant forms. www.companieshouse.co.uk

The Economist

The best single source of information about what is happening in the world. A mainstream publication but one that will take on some big topics from time to time, and one whose take on the new economy is invariably insightful and clear-eyed. www.economist.com

Fast Company

The magazine is monthly and has been an essential read since it started up in 1996. Of late though, the content – whilst still excellent – has been swamped by increasing volumes of advertising. The companion Website is just about the best free site around on the future world of work (it also carries material not found in the magazine). www.fastcompany.com

Financial Times

Of all the dailies, The *Financial Times* provides the best in-depth coverage of organization-related issues. Well worth keeping an eye out for their occasional information technology surveys as well as their monthly e-business magazine Connectis. www.ft.com or www.ft.com/connectis

Fucked Company

An irreverent spoof of *Fast Company* that, like the very best Dilbert cartoons, uses humor as a vehicle for revealing some painful truths about working in the new economy. www.fuckedcompany.com

Harvard Business Review

The most authoritative business monthly on the block. Has tended in the past to be more mainstream than truly groundbreaking in its coverage of business issues. That said, HBR has responded well to the challenge to traditional business thinking posed by the new economy, and recent issues have generally contained two or three relevant articles. Also, if you are interested in getting the lowdown on forthcoming books from Harvard's publishing wing several months before publication, the magazine consistently trails major books with articles from the authors. The Website provides overview of contents of the magazine – no free articles but the executive summaries are there and they are often all you need. www.hbsp.harvard.edu

(The) Information Economy

This Website is overseen by Economist Hal Varian, co-author of *Information Rules*, and lists hundreds of papers, works in progress, and links to other new economy Websites. An almost overwhelming resource but one that hasn't been bettered. http://www.sims.berkeley.edu/resources/infoecon

Internet Business

Just about the best of the recent flurry of new monthlies about doing business on the Internet. Informative mix of case studies, interviews, book extracts, and topical news stories.

Journal of Business Strategies

http://COBA.SHSU.edu/jbs/

The Leadership and Organization Development Journal

The Leadership & Organization Development Journal aims to provide penetrating insights into the expected qualities of leaders in the current climate. It presents research and views on making and developing dynamic leaders, how organizations can and will change, and how leaders can effect this. Contains some excellent links to free articles and information.www.emeraldinsight.com/lodj.htm

Management Link

A one-stop shop containing links to more than 100 key management Websites. www.inst.mgt.org.uk/external/mgt-link

New Scientist

Important science and technology stories will often appear here first. *New Scientist* also gives good coverage to emerging thinking in the scientific community. www.newscientist.com

New Thinking

New Thinking is a weekly, approximately 500-word exploration of the digital age, produced by Gerry McGovern, CEO of Nua and author of *The Caring Economy*. Taking a broad, philosophical view of things, it is written in clear, concise language and delivers some useful comments and ideas. It is available by email and is free. To subscribe to this list, send email to newthinking-request@nua.i.e. with the word *subscribe* in the body of the message.

People Management

The online magazine of the Chartered Institute of Personnel and Development. www.peoplemanagement.co.uk

Sloan Management Review

Since its founding in 1959, MIT's *Sloan Management Review* has covered all management disciplines, although its particular emphasis these days is on corporate strategy, leadership, and management of technology and innovation. Over the years it has featured articles by the likes of Peter Senge, Lester Thurow, James Brian Quinn, Gary Hamel, Thomas Davenport, Christopher Bartlett, Sumantra Ghoshal, John Quelch, Henry Mintzberg, Max Bazerman, and Ed Lawler. http://mitsloan.mit.edu/

Think Tanks

Good starting point for exploring all the UK's major think tanks. www.demos.co.uk/linkuk.htm

Time

Weekly news magazine that gives good, positive coverage to the latest work issues. That said, *Time* is a mainstream publication and so is unlikely to be absolutely at the forefront of business thinking. Nonetheless, it has in recent months carried special features on e-commerce, the future of work, and so on. www.time.com/europe

Wired Magazine

Monthly American magazine that is good at picking up trends about six months before they become trends. www.wired.com/wired/

www.carol.co.uk

A useful port of call for anyone researching a company. Although aimed mainly at potential investors, it is a free corporate on-line service offering one point access to company, providing direct links to over 3000 corporate reports in a single and consistent format.

www.hemscott.co.uk

Useful source of company profiles, lots of data, and the facility to order free annual reports from site.

Ten Steps to Making it Work

This final chapter provides you with 10 key priorities relevant to your organization and its marketplace.

1 Know where you are going
2 Make the best decisions you can
3 Think systemically
4 Learn constantly
5 Innovate
6 Recognize those moments
7 Make it happen
8 Align culture with direction
9 Leadership
10 Make the most of teams.

"We shall not cease from exploration
And the end of all our exploring
Will be to arrive where we started
And know the place for the first time."

T. S. Eliot, Little Gidding

"Optimism is a strategy for making a better future. Because unless you believe that the future can be better, it's unlikely you will step up and take responsibility for making it so. If you assume that there is no hope, you guarantee that there will be no hope. If you assume that . . . there are opportunities to change things, there's a chance you may contribute to making a better world."

Noam Chomsky quoted in Wired magazine, January 1998

By now, it should be pretty apparent that there is no "one best way" for organizations and the people in them to think and act. The following ten points don't attempt to represent absolutely the right priorities for you and your particular organization right now. Some of the points may be irrelevant to your organization and its marketplace; there may be other points not covered.

1   Know where you are going
2   Make the best decisions you can
3   Think systemically
4   Learn constantly
5   Innovate
6   Recognize those moments
7   Make it happen
8   Align culture with direction
9   Leadership
10 Make the most of teams.

So please just recognize the following as a set of generalized principles that will serve most organizations well most of the time. Let's take each in turn.

1. KNOW WHERE YOU ARE GOING

"When a man does not know what harbor he is making for, no wind is the right wind."

Seneca

Successful organizations have the clarity of purpose that provides an over-arching logic for the existence of the organization. While not all writers believe that vision is the most appropriate term for the capacity to imagine and create the future, many recognize that successful organizations have a shared view of the future that stretches the organization beyond its current capabilities. Organizations that have fostered genuinely shared visions can, and do, create their futures, sometimes against overwhelming odds, by mobilizing the resources and commitment of their most valued assets, the people within them.

Shared vision provides the emotional and intellectual energy for the strategic journey to bridge the gap between what is and what could be. Peter Senge, the director of the Center for Organizational Learning at MIT's Sloan School of Management, summarizes this as follows.

"At the heart of building shared vision is the task of designing and evolving ongoing processes in which people at every level of the organization, in every role, can speak from the heart about what really matters to them and be heard."[1]

Vision is deeply paradoxical. It is partly mystical, partly common sense. It is sometimes a picture of the future, sometimes a feeling. It is sometimes fully formed, often not. But it is almost always the ability to see things differently or to integrate disparate and seemingly unrelated information in new ways. Sometimes it is "merely" asking questions that others cannot or will not ask. As John F. Kennedy put it: "some people see things and ask 'why', I see things and ask 'why not?'"

Some organizations (such as Sun Microsystems, Intuit, Monsanto and Amazon.com) talk in terms of visionary leaps into the future. Others plan their way into the future using much more pragmatic tools and techniques, which essentially extrapolate from the current situation. Different perspectives will suit different organizations.

The single most important thing that the leader of a company can do to help it thrive in an era of demanding customers, intense competition, and relentless change is this: help every single person in the company understand the business in the same big-picture terms that the top executives do. The more every employee understands the economics of the company and its industry, its strategy and cost structure, its processes, products, and competitors, the more likely they are to be committed to the chosen route forward.

2. MAKE THE BEST DECISIONS YOU CAN

Decision-making has been defined as the ability to decide on a course of action after due reflection. An article in *Fast Company*[2] suggests four steps to making smarter decisions.

» Wait until the last minute – but not a minute later: if you're not going to do anything differently tomorrow by making a decision today, then don't make it today. Situations change; markets shift. That's not an excuse to procrastinate. But the best decisions are just-in-time decisions.

» Don't be afraid to argue: conflict is good for an organization – as long as it's resolved quickly. Unresolved conflict is a killer. That's why real leaders deal with conflict head-on. They take individual feelings seriously, but then they get beyond those feelings.

» Make the right decision, not the best decision: people can spend months debating the "best" decision without actually arriving at any decision. Every decision involves risk. And if there are 10 ways to do something, eight of them will probably work. So pick one of the eight and get going.

» Disagree – and then commit: not everyone gets a chance to decide, but everyone should have a chance to be heard. Without a doubt, the most vigorous debates yield the best thinking. But once a decision is made, you should not be able to tell who was for it and who was against it. Fully supporting decisions that have been properly made is a condition of employment.

A Harvard Business School article[3] maintains that bad decisions can often be traced back to the way the decisions were made. But sometimes the fault lies not in the decision-making process but rather in the mind of the decision-maker. The way the human brain works can sabotage the choices we make.

Here are eight psychological traps identified in the article that are particularly likely to affect the way people make business decisions.

1 The anchoring trap: this leads us to give disproportionate weight to the first information we receive.
2 The status-quo trap: this biases us toward maintaining the current situation – even when better alternatives exist.
3 The sunk-cost trap: this inclines us to perpetuate the mistakes of the past.
4 The confirming-evidence trap: this leads us to seek out information supporting an existing predilection and to discount opposing information.
5 The framing trap: this occurs when we mis-state a problem, undermining the entire decision-making process.
6 The overconfidence trap: this makes us overestimate the accuracy of our forecasts.
7 The prudence trap: this leads us to be overcautious when we make estimates about uncertain events.
8 The recall-ability trap: this leads us to give undue weight to recent, dramatic events.

The best way to avoid all of the traps is through awareness – forewarned is forearmed.

3. THINK SYSTEMICALLY

"Systems thinking is a discipline for seeing wholes. It is a framework for seeing inter-relationships rather than things, for seeing patterns of change rather than static snapshots."

Peter Senge, The Fifth Discipline

More and more management thinkers and writers are suggesting that scientific theory is a prime source for understanding how organizations and individuals can improve their performance. Most recently, it has been the field of complexity science, sometimes known as chaos theory, which has captured the corporate imagination.

Complexity science is huge in its scope and, well yes, it's quite complex to grasp. It's all too easy to get bound up in technical terminology – phrases like "strange attractors," "emergent capabilities," "states of disequilibrium" etc. abound in the complexity textbooks. At its heart though is the deceptively simple principle that an entity needs to be looked at as a whole "living" system, rather than as a set of individual components.

This insight raises a host of fascinating questions when applied to how we should be tackling the problems we face in organizations. For instance, when analyzing an organizational issue, we have the option of exploring it at a number of levels:

1 Individual
2 Team
3 Inter-group
4 Organizational
5 Inter-organizational
6 Societal
7 International
8 Global.

Let's take the example of the year 2000 American presidential race. Depending on who you listened to, you could have analyzed the problems that occurred with the Florida vote count at the level of:

» voters who were "too stupid to vote properly" (i.e. at the individual level);
» the lack of agreed standards about how to count votes (i.e. an inter-group problem);
» badly designed voting cards (i.e. an organizational issue); and
» the inherent flaws in the whole electoral system (i.e. at the societal level).

Why does this matter? The point is that the level of explanation that we choose determines our view of the causes of an event or problem. It also affects the actions that we take, and the solutions that we employ.

In an organization, an inappropriate intervention at the wrong level can make a problem worse and not better.

Three other points to consider.

1 People tend to pick their favorite level of analysis to explain events, and then behave accordingly. This is often particularly true of external consultants by the way.
2 People are most familiar with, and often prefer, explanations at the individual level of behavior. Trying to change people by sending them on a training course is simpler than changing structures or upgrading technology. However, such explanations all too often are simplistic, inaccurate or incomplete.
3 As a general principle, any organizational problem, for example low productivity or poor team performance, can usefully be analyzed at ever-higher levels of abstraction. By considering it progressively at the individual, group, inter-group and organization levels, a deeper understanding of its causes can be gained. As a result, the tools needed to tackle the problem can be chosen more accurately, and applied more effectively.

Looking at a problem "systemically," to use the jargon, will always yield a better understanding than simply leaping in with all preconceptions blazing. So in future, before we blame a member of staff for cocking up a customer order, maybe we need to ask ourselves whether it truly was their fault.

4. LEARN CONSTANTLY

According to Harvard Business School professor Shoshana Zuboff, "The twenty-first century company has to promote and nurture the capacity to improve and to innovate. That idea has radical implications. It means that learning becomes the axial principle of organizations. It replaces control as the fundamental job of management."[4]

Although the term "learning organization" is now frowned on in some quarters as being old hat, the concept remains both useful and valid. Peter Senge, who did more than anybody to popularize the term[5] back in the early 1990s characterizes learning organizations as places where "people continually expand their capacity to create the results they truly desire, where new and expansive patterns of thinking are nurtured, where collective aspiration is set free, and where people are continually learning how to learn together."

According to Senge, a learning organization is skilled in two particular areas:

» creating, acquiring, and transferring knowledge; and
» modifying its behavior to reflect new knowledge and insights.

For a company, having a positive frame of mind about learning involves the recognition that the skills, knowledge and experience that got it where it is today won't be enough to get it where it wants to be in the future.

John Seely Brown, vice president and chief scientist at the Xerox Corporation, California, has summed up the value of learning thus:

"Learning is important, for both people and organizations. But the real challenge today is unlearning, which is much harder. Each of us has a 'mental model' that we've used over the years to make sense of the world. But the new world of business – built on digital technologies and increasing-returns economics – behaves differently from the world in which we grew up. Before any of us can learn new things, we have to make our current assumptions explicit and find ways to challenge them. This is no academic exercise, and it doesn't come naturally. The harder you fight to hold onto specific assumptions, the more likely there's gold in letting go of them. Step back, reflect – and listen!"[6]

5. INNOVATE

"Companies ... need to build a forgiveness framework – a tolerance for error and failure – into their culture. A company that wants you to come up with a smart idea, implement that idea quickly, and learn in the process has to be willing to cut you some slack."

Jeffrey Pfeffer, Stanford Graduate School of Business[7]

When it comes to assessing the contribution that his staff make to the business, Michael Eisner, head of the Disney Corporation, is unequivocal: "To me, the pursuit of ideas is the only thing that matters," he has said[8]. "You can always find capable people to do almost anything else."

In a working world that grows ever more unpredictable, success will go to people and organizations who are naturally curious, willing to experiment, passionate about their work, and revolutionary in their thinking. Assuming that what works today will work tomorrow is a recipe for the scrap heap.

For a company, successful innovation requires a conscious and explicit commitment and inevitably involves risk. It is best achieved in a "no blame" culture which recognizes that mistakes and failures are the natural and inevitable bedfellows of successful ideas. An innovative organization is typically characterized by informality, the free flow of information, little hierarchy or bureaucracy, and creative interaction within small cross-functional teams and small business units.

Here are a few tips for individuals who wish to hone their capability in this area.

Listen to other people's views

Learn from their experience. Use their intuition and common sense as a source of new ideas. Encourage ideas from all around you. Benchmark other organizations.

Disagree constructively

Innovation depends on relentless self-questioning and the pursuit of continual improvement through constructive argument. Ongoing success is dependent on perpetual dissatisfaction with your performance.

Seek out new experiences

There are many ways to approach this one but here are just three tips on how to change your perspective:

» Try a secondment to another part of the business.

» Ask somebody who has just joined the organization what strikes them as odd about the place; a fresh pair of eyes will often highlight things that you have grown accustomed to and therefore no longer notice.

» Go into newsagents, buy a handful of magazines outside of your immediate specialism, read what's going on in other fields and see if you can make any connections back to your working environment.

Join cross-functional teams whenever you get the chance

Most problems are best solved by inter-disciplinary thinking, which successfully combines and applies different areas of expertise. Perhaps it's time to meet up with those people from production, finance, marketing, and human resources.

Network

Knowledge is the only form of wealth that increases when you give it away. Share your ideas and see what comes back to you.

Capture accidents

The wrong answer is the right answer in search of a different question.

Wait until the last minute

Let your mind drift. Explore tangents. Delay judgment. Postpone criticism.

Don't be impressed by precedent

Anybody who says, "But we've always done it this way" shouldn't be allowed to hold up new ideas.

Continually challenge conventional wisdom

Question all the time. Ask yourself, "What does it mean?" "Why?" "What if?" "How else could I do this?" For example, important questions are:

» why does my organization exist?
» why do we do things and have they any worthwhile purpose? and
» what would we do differently if we started off again from scratch?

6. RECOGNIZE THOSE MOMENTS

Some people call them paradigm shifts. Andy Grove, CEO of Intel, calls them strategic inflection points. They are those moments when our world view changes significantly and irrevocably. Grove describes the process in this edited extract from his book *Only the Paranoid Survive*:[9]

An inflection point occurs where the old strategic picture dissolves and gives way to the new, allowing the business to ascend to new heights. However, if you don't navigate your way through an inflection point, you go through a peak and after the peak the business declines. Put another way, before the strategic inflection point, the industry simply was more like the old. After it, it is more like the new.

So how do we know that a set of circumstances is a strategic inflection point? Most of the time, recognition takes place in stages. First, there is a troubling sense that something is different. Things don't work the way they used to. Customers' attitudes toward you are different. Competitors that you wrote off or hardly knew existed are stealing business from you.

Then there is a growing dissonance between what your company thinks it is doing and what is actually happening inside the bowels of the organization. Eventually, a new framework, a new set of under-standings, a new set of actions emerges. It's as if the group that was lost finds its bearings again. (This could take a year – or a decade.) Last of all, a new set of corporate statements is generated, often by a new set of senior managers.

Given the amorphous nature of an inflection point, how do you know the right moment to take appropriate action, to make the changes that will save your company or your career? Unfortunately, you don't.

But you can't wait until you do know: timing is everything. If you undertake these changes while your company is still healthy, you can save much more of your company's strength, your employees and your strategic position. But that means acting when not everything is known, when the data isn't yet in. Even those who believe in a scientific approach to management will have to rely on instinct and personal judgment. When you're caught in the turbulence of a strategic inflection point, the sad fact is that instinct and judgment are all you've got to guide you through.

But the good news is that even though your judgment got you into this tough position, it can also get you out. It's just a question of training your instincts to pick up a different set of signals. These signals may have been out there all along but you may have ignored them. The strategic inflection point is the time to wake up and listen.

7. MAKE IT HAPPEN

"You have between 30 and 60 days to make an impression as the new leader, . . . to show people that you're doing something. To make a difference, you have one year."
Nina Disesa, chairman and chief creative officer,
McCann-Erickson

"Most people say they're too busy . . . but we all have at least 15 minutes a day. If you use that time well, 15 minutes can matter."
Danny Seo, author

With the publication of *In Search of Excellence* in 1982, Tom Peters and co-author Bob Waterman changed the way organizations thought about themselves. In their book, they identified eight characteristics of excellent companies. Although they subsequently acknowledged that their recipe was incomplete, many of the individual elements remain valid. In particular, their view that management is about taking action (two of their eight characteristics are bias to action and hands-on management) and getting things done still hold good.

Here are some examples of the things that an organization (or an individual come to that) with a high bias to action might do.

» Take risks – go for results.
» Treat failure as an opportunity for positive change.
» Initiate, innovate – don't wait for things to come.
» Persist in the face of obstacles and difficulties.

» Use projects as a tool for delivering rapid results.
» Make connections – network.

Most modern-day managers know that we are living in an age of ever more demanding customers. They want better quality, they want cheaper prices and, above all, they want it now. The bookshop owner who tells a customer that it will take two weeks to order in the book they want is seeing increasing volumes of business going to Internet sites like Amazon. Until very recently, you had physically to go to a bank to get a balance on your account; now it's available on-line, more or less instantly.

There is a four-letter acronym – JFDI – which (in the parental guidance version) stands for "just flipping-well do it." "Making it happen" is about the desire to get on and take action, and to do it to a high standard.

8. ALIGN CULTURE WITH DIRECTION

For as long as the concept of organizational culture has been understood by managers, there has been a misplaced emphasis in organizations seeking to change the way they do things on the notion of "changing the culture."

Let's be clear – there is no such thing as the "right" culture and culture cannot be fostered or installed.

Edgar H. Schein, a professor at the MIT Sloan School of Management, and probably the world's foremost authority on organizational culture, has described the process by which an organizational culture develops in an article he wrote for think tank Demos[10].

"Organizations start with founders and entrepreneurs whose personal assumptions and values gradually create a certain way of thinking and operating, and if their companies are successful, those ways of thinking and operating come to be taken for granted as the 'right' way to run a business. If the founders have the wrong assumptions they never succeed, so it is success that creates organizational culture, not the will of the leaders ... Because cultural assumptions are the product of success, they become more and more stable as the company ages."

Problems emerge if the economic and market environment change as the company ages. The culture of the company can fall out of alignment with environmental realities, resulting in leaders calling for new cultures that are better adapted to the changing environment. However, says Schein, "it is in the nature of culture to remain stable because people's daily routines, their habits of thinking and feeling, their basic assumptions about reality, human nature, truth, etc. are all taken for granted as the only and right way to do things. The proposition that 'we must change our culture' either will be denied or cause levels of anxiety that trigger intense resistance to change."

What then can a company do if current cultural assumptions appear to be dysfunctional or out of alignment with environmental realities? Schein proposes the following set of steps.

1 Start with what the "business problem" is. The organization must understand its mission or its primary task. This issue is not about culture, it is about the organization's reason to be at all.
2 Figure out what needs to be done strategically and tactically to solve the business problem.
3 When there is clear consensus on what needs to be done, examine the existing culture to find out how present tacit assumptions would aid or hinder what needs to be done.
4 Focus on those cultural elements that will help you get to where you need to go. It is far easier to build the strengths of the culture than to change those elements that are dysfunctional or weak.
5 Identify the culture carriers who see the new direction and feel comfortable moving in that direction. Empower specific employees and managers whose assumptions are already in line with the new strategy.
6 Build change teams around the new culture carriers.
7 Adjust the reward, incentive, and control systems to be aligned with the new desired strategy.
8 Ultimately the structures and routine processes of the organization must also be brought into alignment with the desired new directions.

All of this takes a great deal of time and energy on the part of many layers of management, many task forces and change teams. But the motivation to take the time and provide the energy comes from seeing a clear solution to a clear business problem. It does not come from vague protestations about new cultures or new values.

9. LEADERSHIP

"The person who figures out how to harness the collective genius of the people in his or her organization is going to blow the competition away."

Walt Wriston, banker and writer

For twenty years, Richard Pascale was in the faculty of the Stanford Business School. He is now an associate fellow of Oxford University. He is a consultant and a writer.

The following key points are adapted from a letter by Pascale that appeared in the Harvard Business Review[11]. He wrote in response to an earlier article by Ronald Heifetz and Donald Laurie on leadership.

» Leadership occurs only when those in responsible roles consciously endeavor to make happen what wouldn't happen anyway. Heifetz and Laurie call this adaptive work, and it always occurs outside one's comfort zone. Adaptive work is in contrast to technical work, in which executives draw upon a repertoire of pre-existing solutions to address the problems at hand. Technical work is nothing to be ashamed of but it does not require leadership.

» At face value, the distinction between technical work and adaptive work is not difficult to comprehend. The trouble is, with "leadership" being so fashionable these days, many executives don't like to think that they are merely making happen what was going to happen anyway. The idea that most people who occupy executive positions are merely stewards of the inevitable is provocative.

» The authors' second radical idea is to divorce leadership from personality traits. Charisma, boldness, even the capacity to generate organizational purpose are absent from their model. Instead, the central theme shining through their work is mindfulness. They highlight the capacity to discern when traditional solutions are not likely to produce the desired results. That discernment must be followed not by the exercise of personality traits or hard-to-acquire skills but by the discipline necessary to enroll the organization in seeking new solutions.

Noel Tichy, director of a global leadership program at the University of Michigan Business School, describes the role of a leader in this way.

"The most important job for a leader who wants to win in the 21st century is to create more leaders, at more levels of your company, than the competition. This is a job that's too important to outsource: leaders with a proven track record of success – rather than professors or consultants – are the ones to develop more leaders . . . You don't have to be a world-class orator to be a world-class leader. What really counts is the sincerity of your message."

10. MAKE THE MOST OF TEAMS

For most of us in organizations, success often depends on surrounding yourself with the very best people. Working collaboratively is far more likely to deliver good results than working competitively. Somebody once wrote that moving from dependence to independence is a sign of growing up, but that moving from independence to interdependence is a sign of maturity.

There was a story in the papers about four years ago concerning one of the main Whitehall departments that used to run a course called Getting the Most out of your Junior Staff. One of the juniors objected to the title and as a consequence the course was renamed Succeeding with Teams. The content, needless to say, was identical.

If nothing else, this anecdote serves to demonstrate how potent the concept of "team" has become in recent times. There are those who believe that constructive conflict can actually enhance team performance and in turn achieve better decision-making. The authors of a Harvard Business Review article[12] suggested five ways to achieve this.

1 Assemble a team with diverse ages, backgrounds and industry experience.
2 Meet frequently to build familiarity and mutual confidence.

3 Encourage team members to assume roles outside of their obvious functional responsibilities, and so discourage "turf war" thinking.
4 Apply multiple perspectives – role playing, putting yourself in the competitor's shoes etc. This can enable a fresh view of the problem.
5 Actively and overtly manage conflict. Ensure that consensus is real and not just an indication of disengagement.

NOTES

1 Senge, P. (1990) *The Fifth Discipline*, Doubleday, New York.
2 *Fast Company*, October (1998).
3 Hammond, J.S., Keeney, R.L. & Raiffa, H. "The hidden traps in decision making." *Harvard Business Review*, September–October (1998).
4 Zuboff, S. quoted in *Scientific American*, September 1995.
5 Senge, P. (1990) *The Fifth Discipline*, Doubleday, New York.
6 From an article in *Fast Company*, February–March 1997.
7 From an article in the *Fast Take* newsletter, May 9, 2000.
8 Michael Eisner, Disney Corporation, quoted in Syrett, M & Lanniman, J. (1999) *Management Development: Making the Investment Count,* Economist Books, London.
9 Grove, A. (1996) *Only the Paranoid Survive,* HarperBusiness, New York.
10 Schein, E. (1996) "Culture matters." *Demos Quarterly,* 8, Demos.
11 Pascale, R., letter printed in the *Harvard Business Review*, May–June 1997.
12 Eisenhardt, K. M., Kahwajy, J. L. & Bourgeois III, L. J. "How management teams can have a good fight." *Harvard Business Review*, July–August 1997.

Frequently Asked Questions (FAQs)

Q1: What is an organization?

A: There are numerous definitions. Some stress coordination of resources, some emphasize efficiency, while other focus on concepts like community and beliefs. Perhaps the most complete definition is that an organization is a social arrangement for achieving controlled performance in the pursuit of collective goals. See Chapter 2.

Q2: What are the origins of organizations?

A: The roots of modern-day organizations can be traced back to models of Chinese military hierarchy of a good 2000 years' vintage, and quite probably beyond that too, especially if you extend your search parameters into the natural world. See Chapter 3.

Q3: Who are the key figures in organizational theory?

A: They are literally too numerous to mention. Two who were particularly influential in the early days were Henri Fayol and Frederick Taylor (see Chapter 3). More recently, Elliott Jaques and Gareth Morgan have aroused much interest in the business community (see Chapter 2).

Q4: Is there an optimal size or type of organization?

A: No – it totally depends on circumstances. Organizations large or small, old or new, can be highly successful as long as they are tuned into the best practices that apply in their arena of activity. Often success is more about clarity of thinking and commitment than anything else. See Chapter 6.

Q5: What is the average lifespan of an organization?

A: Some organizations have been around for hundreds of years, others have foundered in a matter of months. The average lifespan is probably around the equivalent to a human generation. See the sections titled "Organizations: are the best built to last?" and "Organizations: old is beautiful?" in Chapter 6.

Q6: How does globalization impact on organizations?

A: There are several implications for an organization, no matter what its size, location or industry sector. Most notably, globalization is intensifying levels of competition in many fields. See Chapter 5.

Q7: And what about the impact of new technology?

A: New technology has transformed the working practices of many organizations and has enabled a whole new body of organizational business models to come into being. See Chapter 4.

Q8: How valuable are case studies on organizations that have achieved success in their field?

A: Case studies very rarely produce solutions that can be transplanted wholesale in a different company. Nonetheless, they will always throw up questions and may often suggest a way forward. See Chapter 7.

Q9: So where are organizations heading in the future?

A: Progressive future-oriented organizations are always on the lookout for appropriate tools and lenses for improving future competiveness. Charles Handy has plausibly described a future of "elephants" and "fleas" – very large corporations on the one hand, supported and serviced by external "fleas", small companies, perhaps amounting to only one person, who will offer their expertise on a flexible basis. There will also be significant opportunities for companies of any size that can harness the potential of new and developing technology. See Chapter 6.

Q10: How can I find out more?

A: The problem is not accessing information about organizational theory and practice - there are literally thousands of books and articles published every year. The trick is to distinguish the useful from the irrelevant or derivative. For some recommendations see Chapter 9.

Index

Printed and bound in the UK by
CPI Antony Rowe, Eastbourne

Printed and bound by CPI Group (UK) Ltd, Croydon, CR0 4YY

13/04/2025

14656560-0003